LEAVING CERTIFICATE
ENGLISH HIGHER LEVEL

APPROACH TO ANSWERING PAPER ONE

Format

Paper One is divided into 2 sections and you should allow 2 hours and 50 minutes for this paper.

Section One:	**Comprehending**	**(100 marks)**
Section Two:	**Composing**	**(100 marks)**

On the day of the exam you must answer three questions:

Question A — Comprehension-based questions	**(50 marks)**
Question B — Specific, functional writing tasks	**(50 marks)**
Composition (100 marks)	

Timing

Reading and selecting questions:	10 minutes
Question A:	55 minutes
Question B:	35 minutes
Composition:	1 hour and 10 minutes

Order

Answer questions in the following order:

> Question A
> Question B
> Composition

Remember, Questions A and B *cannot* be answered on the same text.

Question A (55 minutes)

Think of each question as a task that you must perform.

1. First of all, identify the task. Be as clear as you can about exactly what you are being asked to do.

2. Locate and underline the key terms in the question.

3. Where appropriate (unless it specifies 'in your own words'), use specific detail and textual evidence to develop your answer.

4. Note the number of marks allocated per question and use this information as an indication of approximately how long your answer should be.

5. Plan all parts of the question before you begin to write your answer. Some questions may ask about the content or ideas in the text; others about the style of the writing. Some questions may ask for a personal opinion on issues raised in the text. Distinguish between questions that ask for the author's views and those which ask for your own views.

Question B (35 minutes)

Question B is a writing assignment arising out of the text.

1. Your writing will be assessed on your ability to do the following:

   - Engage with the set task.

   - Sustain your response over the entire answer.

   - Manage and control language to achieve clear communication.

2. The language you use in your answer should be appropriate to the task.

3. Note the audience/readership as this will help you to determine the appropriate language for the assignment and the correct format or layout for your answer.

4. The length of your answers will vary according to the task – approximate length will be 1–2 pages. Remember, this is not a composition.

5. It is advisable to read all the texts before beginning to plan your Question B. There may be material here for your chosen writing assignment.

6. Begin a new page in your answer book so that the full effect of the layout is visible to the examiner.

7. The content of your writing assignment is also very important.

   - Plan the points you intend to make.

   - Decide on format/layout.

   - Use appropriate language.

Composition (1 hour and 10 minutes)

The content of your composition must reflect a maturity of approach and a thoughtful response.
When writing your composition, you should consider the following:

   - The purpose of writing

   - The audience

   - The context (newspaper/magazine etc.)

   - Use of appropriate language.

PLAN YOUR COMPOSITION

In an essay, ideas and information cannot be presented all at once; they must be arranged in some order:

   - An introduction

   - The body of the essay

   - The conclusion.

Newspaper and magazine articles should adopt the journalistic conventions of a headline, sub-headings, introduction etc., to give shape to the writing.

The paragraph is the most important unit of thought. In the main body of the essay your paragraphs should be ordered to reflect a sense of movement and progression. Each paragraph should deal with one aspect of the topic. It should have one main idea or topic sentence, together with support or illustrations. Your paragraphs should be connected by the onward thrust of your approach or by transitional words such as 'nevertheless', 'furthermore', 'however' etc. Avoid very long and very short paragraphs. Features of good paragraphs include the following:

- One topic
- Clarity
- Unity – no digressions
- Cohesion – all sentences should relate to the topic sentence.

Remember to use the characteristic techniques of your chosen style.

There are 5 main ways in which language may be used. Each way can be placed in a category. The 5 categories are:

1. Language of information
2. Language of argument
3. Language of persuasion
4. Language of narration
5. Aesthetic use of language.

Category	Characteristics	Purpose
1. **Information**	Clarity Order	To show To inform
2. **Argument** (a rational, ordered presentation)	Order Reason Logic	To demonstrate To make a case for To convince
3. **Persuasion** (one new dimension here – emotive; to convince is more central.) Rhetorical devices should be considered in this category.	Clarity Emotion	To convince To persuade
4. **Narration** (A narrative works when the reader is convinced by the world depicted in it. It comes alive as we read.)	Truth Realism	To involve/ engage/ captivate the reader
5. **Aesthetic**: This is not really a separate category but is found throughout the other styles of writing. In every category we enjoy or note the beauty/rhythm/energy of words and this is characteristic of the aesthetic dimension of language to be found in literature.		

APPROACH TO ANSWERING PAPER TWO

Format

This part of the paper is divided into three sections: Section I **(The Single Text)**, Section II **(The Comparative Study)**, and Section III **(Poetry)**. Each of these sections has to be attempted. Remember you *must* answer on Shakespearean Drama, either as a Single Text or as an element in the Comparative Study. You should allow 3 hours and 20 minutes for this paper.

Section I (The Single Text): 60 marks

Section II (The Comparative Study): 70 marks

Section III (Poetry): 70 marks

Timing

Reading and selecting questions: 15 mins

Section I (The Single Text, 60 marks) 55 mins

Section II (The Comparative Study, 70 marks) 1 hour and 5 minutes

Section III (Poetry, 70 marks) 1 hour and 5 minutes

Section I (The Single Text, 60 marks) 55 mins

You will be required to attempt a question on one of the prescribed Single Texts. Two questions will be set on each of the texts.

Section II (The Comparative Study, 70 marks) 1 hour and 5 minutes

You are required to answer one question from this section. Normally two questions are set on each of the modes of comparison.

Section III (Poetry: 70 marks) 1 hour and 5 minutes

Poetry is worth 70 marks on the Higher Level paper. Fifty marks are available for seen poetry and 20 marks for unseen poetry. It is extremely important that you do everything you can to maximise your chances on the day of the examination. The first thing that you need to do is to become familiar with the marking scheme.

The Marking Scheme

On a general level, the corrector will be looking for four different qualities in your answers in Paper Two.

1. The first of these is *Clarity of Purpose*. Here, the corrector will want to see that your answer engages with the question asked. This is worth 30 per cent of the available marks. In order to get the full marks available for Clarity of Purpose, you would have to:

    *   Provide an original and fresh answer. (Slavishly learnt-off material can often damage your prospects in the exam.)

    *   Show that you understand the genre you are writing about. This means, for example, that you demonstrate how drama differs from other areas of the course. While you don't want to overdo it, a technical knowledge of the different genres can help here. Remember that in the comparative section you must compare and contrast the texts that you have studied.

    *   Focus on what the question is asking you to do. If you were asked to explain why you liked or disliked the work of a certain poet, you would have to state explicitly why you liked his/her poetry. It would not be acceptable simply to say, 'I like her poetry.' You must always justify your statements by providing examples from the poems on the course. According to the Chief

Examiner's Report of 2005 'answers were most successful where candidates made good use of the text to reinforce a point of view or response'.

Most marks are lost for Clarity of Purpose by:

- Retelling the story of the text. This is known as paraphrasing. Remember, you are expected to know the content of your texts. The content of the text is only useful insofar as it illustrates a point that addresses the question asked. In reference to the poetry section of the paper, the Chief Examiner's Report in 2001 specifically mentioned this point, saying that candidates should be aware that, while questions on poetry will require them to come to terms with the content of poems, they may also require them to deal with the language of poetry. The easiest way to avoid paraphrasing is to deal with the text in a global sense. Paragraphs that concentrate too much on the events in a novel, play or film lend themselves to paraphrasing.

- Reproducing an essay that you have learnt off by heart that does not address the question fully.

2. The second area that the corrector will consider is the ***Coherence of Delivery***. Here, the corrector wants to see an ability to sustain your response throughout the entire answer. This is worth 30 per cent of the available marks.

In order to gain the full 15 marks available for Coherence of Delivery, you need to sustain your essay in a manner that demonstrates:

- Continuity of argument: in other words, your ideas need to follow on from one another.

- Management of ideas: you must control the manner in which you present your ideas in an essay. The easiest way to ensure this is to write in focused paragraphs. A focused paragraph deals with one aspect of the question. This one aspect can be technical, e.g. use of rhythm, or thematic, e.g. death, love etc. Remember, you would have to tie all these in with the question asked. In a poetry essay that required a personal response, a paragraph focusing on the theme of death would have to show how the poet's treatment of the subject impacted on you, the reader.

- Engagement with the texts: you must show that you understand how the texts function and achieve their impact. It is not simply enough to know what the text is about. A statement such as 'this is a dramatic scene' is useless unless you show how the scene is dramatic.

You will lose marks available for Coherency of Delivery if you:

- Fail to shape your argument. Remember, your essay must have a beginning, a middle and a conclusion.

- Write in disorganised paragraphs that lack focus. Remember, the definition of a paragraph is a group of sentences dealing with one idea.

- Use the wrong register. Your tone of voice and the type of language that you use are important aspects of your essay. While you should try to write in a natural style, the fact that you are writing an essay implies a certain degree of formality.

3. The third area that the corrector will concern him/herself with is ***Efficiency of Language*** use. The corrector will want to see clear evidence of your ability to manage and control your language, so as to achieve clear communication. This is worth 30 per cent of the available marks. If you want to obtain the full 15 marks available for Efficiency of Language, you must:

- Control your expression. This means that your sentences should flow naturally. Avoid very long sentences. If something can be said clearly in a short sentence, don't try to make it more complicated. You must ensure that the syntax (word order) of your sentences is logical.

- Ensure that your paragraphs are structured correctly. As previously stated, you must write in ordered paragraphs that work together to answer the question. Try to link your paragraphs where possible.

- Use lively, interesting language and phrasing. Try to vary your sentence length and avoid repetition of words and phrases. Once again, knowledge of the technical aspects of the author or director's work can help make your language more interesting.

You will lose marks for your language if you:

- Fail to write clear and logical sentences that make complete sense to the person reading them. The golden rule is, if you are slightly unclear about what your sentence is saying, then the person reading it will be completely lost.

- Use learnt-off material that does not logically fit in with the rest of your argument or address the question asked.

- Write an essay that does not contain ordered paragraphs.

4. The final area that the marking scheme addresses is called *Accuracy of Mechanics*. This is basically spelling and grammar. Ten per cent of the available marks are given for this.

There are 5 marks available for grammar and spelling. While the corrector will not punish you for obvious slips of the hand, you will be penalised for poor spelling and grammar. If your grammar and spelling are very weak, they will obviously impact on other areas of the marking scheme.

Leaving Certificate English (Higher Level) Progress Tracker

Tick when you have completed a question and again when you have completed a full paper.

Paper 1 is divided into two sections: Section I – Comprehending and Section II – Composing. You should answer three questions in Paper 1. Of these, you must answer one Question A and one Question B from Section I, and one question from Section II. Note: Questions A and B cannot be answered on the same text. Paper 1, Section 1 has not contained a Text 4 since 2002, but it is included here for tracking purposes.

Paper 2 is divided into three sections: Section 1 – The Single Text, Section II – The Comparative Study and Section III – Poetry. Candidates should answer one question from Section 1, one question from Section 2, one question on the Unseen Poem from Section 3, and one question on Prescribed Poetry from Section 3.

	2009	2008	2007	2006	2005	2004	2003	2002	2001	SEC Sample	Sample 1	Sample 2	Sample 3	Sample 4
Paper 1														
Section 1 – Comprehending														
Text 1														
Question A														
Question B														
Text 2														
Question A														
Question B														
Text 3														
Question A														
Question B														
Text 4														
Question A														
Question B														
Section 2 – Composing														
Question 1														
Question 2														
Question 3														
Question 4														
Question 5														
Question 6														
Question 7														

	2009	2008	2007	2006	2005	2004	2003	2002	2001	SEC Sample	Sample 1	Sample 2	Sample 3	Sample 4
Paper 2														
Section 1 – Single Text														
Question A														
Question B														
Question C														
Question D														
Question E														
Section 2 – Comparative Study														
Question A														
Question B														
Section 3 – Poetry														
Question A – Unseen Poem														
Question B – Prescribed Poetry														
Paper Complete														

8

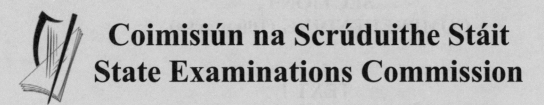

Coimisiún na Scrúduithe Stáit
State Examinations Commission

LEAVING CERTIFICATE EXAMINATION, 2009

English – Higher Level – Paper I

Total Marks: 200

Wednesday, 3 June – Morning, 9.30 – 12.20

- This paper is divided into two sections,
  Section I COMPREHENDING and Section II COMPOSING.
- The paper contains **three** texts on the general theme of DECISIONS.
- Candidates should familiarise themselves with each of the texts before beginning their answers.

- Both sections of this paper (COMPREHENDING and COMPOSING) must be attempted.
- Each section carries 100 marks.

SECTION I – COMPREHENDING

- Two Questions, A and B, follow each text.
- Candidates must answer a Question A on one text and a Question B on a different text. Candidates must answer only one Question A and only one Question B.
- **N.B.** Candidates may NOT answer a Question A and a Question B on the same text.

SECTION II – COMPOSING

- Candidates must write on **one** of the compositions 1 – 7.

SECTION I
COMPREHENDING (100 marks)

TEXT 1
Decisions for Society

This text is taken from *Head to Head*, a series of public debates, published in April 2008 in *The Irish Times*; it consists of two extracts in response to the question:

Should Zoos be Closed?

NO, according to Veronica Chrisp (Head of Marketing at Dublin Zoo) who believes zoos connect us to the natural world.

If anybody could witness the look of amazement and wonder on the face of a six-year-old child as he, or she, sees an elephant, a snake or a gorilla for the very first time, it is unlikely that zoos would ever again be put on the defensive.

Of course, in our culture, the very word *zoo* has negative connotations – often evoking ideas of bored animals kept in Victorian menageries for the benefit of an unappreciative audience. Nothing could be further from the truth. Animals in zoos live enriched lives: they are fit and healthy, able to breed and raise their young. They can be observed in naturalistic spaces with vegetation and water features that reflect their native habitat and are designed with the animals' physical, psychological and social needs in mind. The designers of Dublin Zoo's Kaziranga forest trail, for example, sought inspiration from the wild before ever setting pen to paper. Two healthy elephant calves later, the habitat is proving a delight for elephants and their visitors alike.

The ethical and well-managed zoo has a vital role in our society: as a living classroom,

(continued on page 3)

YES, according to Bernie Wright (Press Officer of the Alliance for Animal Rights) who believes zoos will always be prisons for animals.

A zoo is simply a collection of animals. It makes money by attracting paying visitors. The quality of life for the animals varies from totally inadequate to barely adequate.

In 2008, Dublin Zoo sits on roughly 60 acres. It boasts such habitats as African plains, fringes of the Arctic, rainforests, the Kaziranga forest trail, and shops and restaurants. All of this, and 600 animals ranging from tigers, elephants and chimps to red pandas, hardly seems like a natural environment. To quote the zoo, it invites visitors to "go wild in the heart of the city". It's a pity the animals cannot do the same. Indeed, it is well documented that elephants can roam more than 40 miles in a day in their natural surroundings.

Most animals on display in zoos are not threatened by extinction, yet captive breeding programmes which endeavour to save species are one of the most common reasons that zoos use to justify their existence. When asked how many animals have been reintroduced back into the wild by Dublin Zoo since the 1800s, the answer was "we have none in the records but

(continued on page 3)

NO (continued)	YES (continued)

conservation centre, animal sanctuary, centre of excellence in animal husbandry, science and research, and a major visitor attraction. And in order to remind people of the joy of the natural world, and to encourage and inspire visitors to understand wildlife, the zoo offers a really great day out for all.

Modern zoos are managed by caring professionals who devote their lives to the welfare of animals and to understanding their needs; they adhere to strict codes of practice in animal welfare laid down by European and global associations.

More than 900,000 people visited Dublin Zoo in 2007. All age groups, nationalities and different walks of life were represented – 50,000 of them were schoolchildren who visited as part of their formal education.

Imagine the void left if the zoo was closed. Who would tell children about how elephants communicate, why monkeys hang by their tails or why flamingos are pink? How wonderful that they can see a real elephant or a zebra, or even a meerkat, without even having to switch on the television.

possibly a golden lion tamarin". Strangely, there are no statistics for released animals.

The focus of zoos is on human entertainment rather than education. They tend to be home to crowd-pleasers – animals that are cute, or massive, or funny, or ferocious. The Alliance for Animal Rights' observations show that even if learning material is available, most zoo-goers disregard it. Children, especially, rush from one exhibit to another, pausing only if animals are being fed or performing cute tricks. Good wildlife television programmes today can show normal behaviour of animals in their natural surrounds. Alternatively, there are safari jobs or holidays. We do not need to confine animals in zoos to learn.

Some animals might live longer in zoos, but at what price? Elephants in captivity display chronic health problems. Other animals just go mad. Unnaturally housed or insane animals cannot be representative of their species. It is morally unacceptable to keep any being in an environment where natural instincts are continuously frustrated – the enclosure becomes a prison. I urge anyone who visits a zoo to really look into an animal's eyes. Do they deserve life imprisonment without ever committing a crime?

N.B.   Candidates may NOT answer Question A and Question B on the same text.

Questions A and B carry 50 marks each.

QUESTION A

(i)   Based on your reading of the above text, outline the views of Veronica Chrisp and Bernie Wright on **animal welfare in zoos**.   (15)

(ii)   Join the debate.
        Having considered the views expressed in the text, do **you** think zoos should be closed?
        Give reasons for your decision.   (15)

(iii)   Select **four features** of argumentative and/or persuasive writing evident in the text and comment on their effectiveness. Refer to the text in support of your answer.   (20)

QUESTION B
"Go wild in the heart of the city".
Imagine you are making a cartoon film (featuring animals as characters) **either** to promote **or** oppose zoos. Write the **script of a scene (in dialogue form)** between two of the animal characters.

(50)

Narritive piece. Dialogue.
"I" personnal.
Setting up story.

Personal Decisions

This text is taken from a short story by Australian writer David Malouf entitled *The Valley of Lagoons*. In this extract, a bookish young teenager longs to join his mates on a hunting trip to the mysterious Valley of Lagoons. The story is set in Brisbane, Australia.

My father was not a hunting man. When he and my mother first came here in the late nineteen thirties, he'd been invited out, when August came round, on a hunting party to the Lagoons. It was a courtesy, an act of neighbourliness extended to a newcomer, if only to see how he might fit in. "Thanks Gerry," I imagine him saying in his easy way. "Not this time I reckon. Ask me again next year, eh?" And he had said that again the following year, and the year after, until they stopped asking. My father wasn't being stand-offish or condescending. It was simply that hunting, and the grand rigmarole, as he saw it, of gun talk and game talk and dog talk, was not his style.

He had been a soldier in New Guinea and had seen enough perhaps, for one lifetime, of killing. It was an oddness in him that was accepted like any other, humorously, and was perhaps not entirely unexpected in a man who had more books in his house than could be found in the county library.

As the town's only solicitor, he was a respected figure. He was liked. My mother too was an outsider and, despite heavy hints, had not joined the sewing circle and jam-and-chutney-makers.

After more than twenty years in the district, my father had never been to the Lagoons, and till I was sixteen I had not been there either, except in the dreamtime of my own imaginings. When I was in third grade at primary school, it was the magic of the name itself that drew me. But it was not marked on the wall-map in our classroom and I could not find it in any atlas which gave it the status of a secret place. It had a history but only in the telling: in stories I heard from fellows in the playground at school, or from their older brothers at the barbershop.

descriptive

Just five hours south off a good dirt highway, it was where all the river systems in our quarter of the state have their rising: the big rain-swollen streams that begin in a thousand thread-like runnels and falls in the rainforests, then plunge and gather and flow wide-banked and muddy-watered to the coast. It was the place where the leisurely watercourses make their way inland across plains stacked with anthills and break up and lose themselves in the mudflats and swamps.

flow · *adjetives. imagery.*

Each year in the first week of August, my friend Braden's father, Wes McGowan, got up a hunting party. I was always invited. My father after a good deal of humming and ha-ing and using my mother as an excuse, would tell me I was too young and decline to let me go. But I knew he was uneasy about it, and all through the last weeks of July, as talk in the town grew, I waited in the hope he might relent.

When the day of the hunt came I would get up early, pull on a sweater against the cold and, in the misty half-light just before dawn, jog down the deserted main street, past the last service station at the edge of town, to the river park where the McGowans' truck would be waiting, piled high with tarpaulins, bedrolls, cook-pots, and Braden settled among them with two Labrador retrievers at his feet.

Old Wes McGowan and Henry Denkler, who was also the town mayor, would be out stretching their legs, stamping their boots on the frosty ground or bending to inspect the tyres. The older McGowan boys, Stuart and Glen, would be squatting on their heels over a smoke. When the second vehicle drew up with Matt Riley and his nephew, Jem, a second inspection would be made of the tyres and the load and then with all the rituals of meeting done, they would climb into the cabin of the truck, and I would be left standing to wave them off; and then jog slowly back home.

The break came in the year after I turned sixteen. When I went for the third or fourth year running to tell my father that the McGowans had offered to take me out to the Lagoons and to ask if I could go, he surprised me by looking up over the top of his glasses and saying, "That's up to you, son. You're old enough, I reckon, to make your own decisions". It was to be Braden's last trip before he went to university. "So," said my father quietly, though he already knew the answer, "what's it to be?"
"I'd really like to go," I told him.

"Good," he said, not sounding regretful. "I want you to look out and be careful, that's all. Braden's a sensible enough young fellow. But your mother will worry her soul case out till you're home again."
What he meant was, *he* would.

Just before sun-up, the McGowans' truck swung uphill to where I was waiting with my duffel bag and bedroll on our front veranda. Behind me, the lights were on in our front room and my mother was there in her dressing gown, with a mug of tea to warm her hands, just inside the screen door. I was glad the others could not see her, and hoped she would not come out at the last moment to kiss me or tuck my scarf into my windcheater. But in fact, "Look after Braden," was all she said as I waved and shouted "See you" over my shoulder and took three leaps down to the front gate.

N.B. **Candidates may NOT answer Question A and Question B on the same text.**

Questions A and B carry 50 marks each.

QUESTION A

(i) David Malouf evokes a strong sense of place in this extract from his short story. What impression do you get of the Australian town and its people? Support your answer with reference to the text. (15)

(ii) Do you think the boy has a good relationship with his parents? Give reasons for your answer. (15)

(iii) Identify and comment on **four** features of narrative and/or descriptive writing evident in this text. Support your answer by illustration from the text. (20)

QUESTION B
"You're old enough, I reckon, to make your own decisions."
Write a short **speech** in which you attempt to persuade a group of parents that older teenagers should be trusted to make their own decisions. (50)

TEXT 3

The Decisive Moment

The following text consists of a visual and written element. The visual part is a selection of photographs by Henri Cartier-Bresson. The written element is an extract from an essay entitled "Creating the Decisive Moment" by Frank Van Riper.

① Man jumping a puddle, Paris. 1932

② Friendship, New Jersey. 1947

③ Solitude, Downtown, New York. 1947

④ The Unemployed read the Want Ads, Los Angeles. 1947

Creating the Decisive Moment

Henri Cartier-Bresson, (1908-2004), the legendary photographer, coined the term "the decisive moment" to refer to photography's unique ability to freeze time, to capture moments in an instant, be it a fleeting emotion between two lovers, peak sports action or tragedy amid war and upheaval. He believed that there was nothing in the world that did not have a decisive moment and there was just a creative fraction of a second for a photographer to know when to click the camera.

Part of being able to capture the decisive moment is practice and, just as in fishing, it requires great patience and flawless reflexes. I've learned that sometimes the best moments happen after or before an actual event. The first instance that comes to mind is trying to make a telling picture of a child blowing out birthday candles. You wait for the child to perform and most often you'll get a passable photo of a kid with billowing cheeks blowing out candles. But with more experience you wait for the instant just after the candles go out, when the child looks up from the cake, his or her face flush with excitement and achievement amid a wreath of candle smoke.

One of my favourite shots during my time as a children's photographer was of twin toddler boys sitting side by side on a couch in their parents' living room. During the shoot I asked the mother to place her older son's electric guitar – something they were never allowed to touch – in their lap. The ecstatic looks on the boys' faces – the decisive moment, to be sure – was the best picture of the session. The smallest thing, the little human detail, can be a great subject and when you capture it and everything else falls together, it is a wonderful feeling.

Photography is unique among the visual arts, not only because a photograph cannot be created from memory, but because the subject of the photograph – and not really the photographer – determines absolutely what the depiction will be. "Photography shows us things that lie beyond our imagination and compel our amazement because they really happened," said writer David Jenkins. That's why I cringe to hear people dismissing the idea of the decisive moment as outmoded and irrelevant today because a picture or photograph can now be patched together from different digital elements. Sure it can. Just don't call it photography.

N.B. Candidates may NOT answer Question A and Question B on the same text.

Questions A and B carry 50 marks each.

QUESTION A

(i)   From your reading of this text what do you understand by the term "the decisive moment"? Refer to both the **written and visual text** in support of your answer. (15)

(ii) Select **three** features of the author's style in the **written** element of the text and comment on their effectiveness. Support your answer with reference to the **written** text. (15)

(iii) Write a personal response to the visual image in Text 3 that makes the greatest impact on you.
[You might consider the subject matter, setting, mood, caption, relevancy, photographic qualities/technique, etc.] (20)

QUESTION B

"…photography's unique ability to freeze time…"
Imagine your art teacher is compiling a photographic exhibition to reflect the lives of young people today. She has asked students to suggest images they would like included. Write a **letter** to your art teacher proposing **five** images that you believe should be included and give reasons for your decision in each case. (50)

SECTION II
COMPOSING (100 marks)

Write a composition on **any one** of the following.

Each composition carries 100 marks.

The composition assignments below are intended to reflect language study in the areas of information, argument, persuasion, narration, and the aesthetic use of language.

1. "…a living classroom…"   (TEXT 1)

    Write an article (serious and/or light-hearted) for a school magazine about your experience of education over the last number of years.

2. "…a good deal of humming and ha-ing…"   (TEXT 2)

    Write an opinion piece for a popular magazine entitled "Indecision – my own and other people's".

3. "…the decisive moment…"   (TEXT 3)

    Write a short story in which the central character is faced with making an important decision.

4. "…science and research…"   (TEXT 1)

    Write a persuasive speech in praise of science and technology.

5. "…a respected figure."   (TEXT 2)

    Write a newspaper article on some of today's respected public figures, exploring the qualities that make them worthy of respect.

6. "…the dreamtime of my own imaginings."   (TEXT 2)

    Write a personal essay on the topic of daydreams.

7. **Write a short story in which a photograph, or a set of photographs, plays a part in the plot. Your story may be prompted by one or more of the photographs in TEXT 3.**

M.12C

2009

Coimisiún na Scrúduithe Stáit
State Examinations Commission

LEADING CERTIFICATE EXAMINATION, 2009

English - Higher Level - Paper 2

Total Marks: 200

Time: 3 hours 20 minutes

Candidates must attempt the following:-

- **ONE** question from SECTION I – The Single Text   55
- **ONE** question from SECTION II – The Comparative Study   1hr 5
- **ONE** question on the Unseen Poem from SECTION III – Poetry   20 | 1hr 5
- **ONE** question on Prescribed Poetry from SECTION III – Poetry   45

N.B. Candidates must answer on Shakespearean Drama.

They may do so in SECTION I, The Single Text (*Macbeth*)

or in SECTION II, The Comparative Study (*Macbeth, The Tempest*).

INDEX OF SINGLE TEXTS

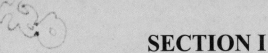

SECTION I

THE SINGLE TEXT (60 marks)

Candidates must answer **one** question from this section (**A – E**).

A   CAT'S EYE – Margaret Atwood

   (i)   "There are no villains in *Cat's Eye*, only vulnerable human beings."

            Write a response to this statement, referring to **one or more** of the characters
            from the novel.

OR

   (ii)   *"Cat's Eye* is concerned with the struggle of human beings for survival."

            Discuss this view, supporting your answer by reference to the text.

B   REGENERATION – Pat Barker

   (i)   "Rivers is changed utterly by his contact with his patients."

            Write a response to this statement. Support your answer with the aid of suitable
            reference to the text.

OR

   (ii)   Write the text of a talk you would give to your class outlining the factors that
            made *Regeneration* an interesting novel for you to read.

            Your talk should include detailed reference to the text.

C   JANE EYRE – Charlotte Brontë

(i)   "Jane Eyre's experiences throughout the novel expose the divisions in her society."
Discuss this statement, supporting your answer with the aid of suitable reference to the text.

OR

(ii)   "The effectiveness of Brontë's imagery and symbolism heightens the impact of *Jane Eyre*."
Write a response to this statement. Support your views by reference to the text.

D   THE CRUCIBLE – Arthur Miller

(i)   To what extent is John Proctor a heroic character in *The Crucible*?
Support the points you make by reference to the text.

OR

(ii)   A Leaving Certificate student once asked: "How relevant is *The Crucible* to the modern reader?" Write the text of a talk you would give in answer to the question.
Your talk should include detailed reference to the play.

E   MACBETH – William Shakespeare

(i)   "Macbeth's murder of Duncan has horrible consequences both for Macbeth himself and for Scotland."
Write a response to this statement. You should refer to the play in your answer.

OR

(ii)   "*Macbeth* has all the ingredients of compelling drama."
Write a response to this statement, commenting on **one or more** of the ingredients which, in your opinion, make *Macbeth* a compelling drama.

SECTION II

THE COMPARATIVE STUDY (70 marks)

Candidates must answer **one** question from **either A** – Theme or Issue **or B** – The Cultural Context.

In your answer you may not use the text you have answered on in **SECTION I** – The Single Text.

N.B. The questions use the word **text** to refer to all the different kinds of texts available for study on this course, i.e. novel, play, short story, autobiography, biography, travel writing, and film. The questions use the word **author** to refer to novelists, playwrights, writers in all genres, and film-directors.

A   THEME OR ISSUE

1. "Important themes are often expressed in key moments in texts."

    Compare how the authors of the comparative texts studied by you used key moments to heighten your awareness of an important theme.   (70)

OR

2. *(a)* Choose a theme from **one** text you have studied as part of your comparative course and say how it helped maintain your interest in the text.   (30)

    (b) Compare how the theme you have dealt with in part *(a)* is treated by the authors of **two other texts** from your comparative course to maintain the reader's interest.   (40)

B   THE CULTURAL CONTEXT

1. "The main characters in texts are often in conflict with the world or culture they inhabit."

    In the light of the above statement, compare how the main characters interact with the cultural contexts of the texts you have studied for your comparative course.

    (70)

OR

2. "Understanding the cultural context of a text allows you to see how values and attitudes are shaped."

    (a)   Show how this statement applies to **one** of the texts on your comparative course.

    (30)

    (b)   Compare the way in which values and attitudes are shaped in **two other texts** on your comparative course. Support the comparisons you make by reference to the texts.

    (40)

SECTION III
POETRY (70 marks)

Candidates must answer **A** – Unseen Poem **and B** – Prescribed Poetry.

A   UNSEEN POEM (20 marks)

Answer **either** Question **1 or** Question **2**.

In this poem, Anne Carson recalls her father and, in particular, his final illness during which he goes back to being like a child again.

FATHER'S OLD BLUE CARDIGAN

Now it hangs on the back of the kitchen chair
where I always sit, as it did
on the back of the kitchen chair where he always sat.

I put it on whenever I come in,
as he did, stamping
the snow from his boots.

I put it on and sit in the dark.
He would not have done this.
Coldness comes paring down from the moonbone in the sky.

His laws were a secret.
But I remember the moment at which I knew
he was going mad inside his laws.

He was standing at the turn of the driveway when I arrived.
He had on the blue cardigan with the buttons done up all the way to the top.
Not only because it was a hot July afternoon

but the look on his face –
as a small child who has been dressed by some aunt early in the morning
for a long trip

on cold trains and windy platforms
will sit very straight at the edge of his seat
while the shadows like long fingers

over the haystacks that sweep past
keep shocking him
because he is riding backwards.

---

1.   Write a response to the above poem, highlighting the impact it makes on you.   (20)

OR

2.   (a)   What impression of Anne Carson's father do you get from reading this poem?
            Support your view by reference to the poem.   (10)
      (b)   Briefly describe the mood or feeling you get from reading this poem and
            illustrate your answer from the text.   (10)

B PRESCRIBED POETRY (50 marks)

Candidates must answer **one** of the following questions (**1 – 4**).

1. "**Derek Walcott** explores tensions and conflicts in an inventive fashion."

    Do you agree with this assessment of his poetry? Write a response, supporting your points with the aid of suitable reference to the poems you have studied.

2. "**John Keats** presents abstract ideas in a style that is clear and direct."

    To what extent do you agree or disagree with this assessment of his poetry? Support your points with reference to the poetry on your course.

3. "**John Montague** expresses his themes in a clear and precise fashion."

    You have been asked by your local radio station to give a talk on the poetry of John Montague. Write out the text of the talk you would deliver in response to the above title. You should refer to both style and subject matter. Support the points you make by reference to the poetry on your course.

4. "**Elizabeth Bishop** poses interesting questions delivered by means of a unique style."

    Do you agree with this assessment of her poetry? Your answer should focus on both themes and stylistic features. Support your points with the aid of suitable reference to the poems you have studied.

Coimisiún na Scrúduithe Stáit
State Examinations Commission

LEAVING CERTIFICATE EXAMINATION, 2008

English – Higher Level – Paper I

Total Marks: 200

Wednesday, 4th June – Morning, 9.30 – 12.20

- This paper is divided into two sections,
  Section I COMPREHENDING and Section II COMPOSING.
- The paper contains **three** texts on the general theme of IDENTITY.
- Candidates should familiarise themselves with each of the texts before beginning their answers.

- Both sections of this paper (COMPREHENDING and COMPOSING) must be attempted.
- Each section carries 100 marks.

SECTION I – COMPREHENDING

- Two Questions, A and B, follow each text.
- Candidates must answer a Question A on one text and a Question B on a different text. Candidates must answer only one Question A and only one Question B.
- **N.B.** Candidates may NOT answer a Question A and a Question B on the same text.

SECTION II – COMPOSING

- Candidates must write on **one** of the compositions 1 – 7.

SECTION 1
COMPREHENDING (100 marks)

TEXT 1

TEENAGE IDENTITY

This text is adapted from Jon Savage's book, "Teenage, the Creation of Youth, 1875 – 1945", in which he traces the history of the modern teenager.

Modern teenagers are the ultimate psychic match for the times: living in the now, pleasure-seeking, product-hungry, embodying the new global society.

But where did teenagers come from? Teenage culture is not a modern phenomenon. Teenagers did not simply appear fully formed when the term entered everyday use in the 1940s. In fact the whole business machinery of modern youth culture – hit songs, heavily marketed products, commercial venues for dancing – was up and running, particularly in America before the 20th century even began.

The phrase "juvenile delinquent" was coined in America around 1810 in response to teenage gangs who, with their own dress codes, rituals and street-corner poses, were filling newspapers and populating novels. *The Daily Graphic* described an 1890s London gang member as having "a peculiar muffler twisted around the neck, a cap set rakishly forward, well over the eyes, and trousers very tight at the knee and loose at the foot". In 1899 Clarence Rook's South London novel *The Hooligan Nights* featured a highly strung 17-year-old male protagonist with a darting gaze "like the eyes of a bird perpetually prepared for conflict". It is hard not to imagine Victorian adults keeping away from him on the top deck of a tram.

It was the American social psychologist G. Stanley Hall who coined the term "adolescence" in 1898 and defined it as "a period of ten years, from twelve or fourteen to twenty-one or twenty-five".

Characterising it as a period of "storm and stress", he advised adults to treat adolescents with sympathy, appreciation and respect before subjecting them to the relentless responsibilities of adult industrial life. The term "generation" up to this had been used to describe "all men living more or less in the same time" but now it began to refer to "the new generation", the idea of youth as a separate class, with its own institutions and values.

In Britain this took the form of small earnest groups such as the Woodcraft Folk who offered young people contact with nature and loyalty to the community. Their counterparts in Germany were the Wandervogel, adolescents who rebelled against authoritarian schooling before World War One by hiking, camping and singing folk songs. In France there were the Zazous who listened to jazz and swing, wore extravagant clothes and flirted like there was no tomorrow.

The decade of the Roaring Twenties introduced an international party scene of pleasure-seeking bright young people, similar to today's celebs, Paris Hilton and Lindsay Lohan, who saturate our own media. Bobby-soxers, the female swing fans with their sporty outfits and dance-ready shoes, screamed en masse for Frank Sinatra and laid the groundwork for gyrating rock'n'rollers, Elvis Presley fans and "Beatlemania".

In 1944 the magazine *Seventeen* was published, a fashion and pop magazine aimed at high-school girls. It was a landmark crystallization of teenage identity. Now teenagers were neither adolescents nor juvenile delinquents. They were a separate consumer grouping. "*Seventeen* is your magazine," proclaimed the first issue. "It is interested only in you and everything that concerns, excites, annoys, pleases or perplexes you."

1945 was Year Zero, the start of a new era after the atrocities of World War Two and the unleashing of the ultimate terror weapon, the atomic bomb. The best placed group to flourish in a post-war era were the young. "Their lives are lived principally in hope," Aristotle had once written of the young, while for Stanley Hall, adolescence was nothing less than "a new birth".

The future would be *Teenage*.

N.B. Candidates may NOT answer Question A and Question B on the same text.

Questions A and B carry 50 marks each.

QUESTION A

(i)   "Teenage culture is not a modern phenomenon". Give **three** pieces of evidence that the writer, Jon Savage, uses to support this statement.   (15)

(ii)   Comment on **three** features of the style of writing which contribute to making this an interesting and informative text. Refer to the text in support of your answer.   (15)

(iii)   Do you think the writer of this text is sympathetic to the modern teenager? Give reasons for your view with reference to the text.   (20)

QUESTION B

Write a letter to Jon Savage **responding to this extract** from his book **and giving your own views** on today's teenage culture.   (50)

TEXT 2

FALSE IDENTITY?

This text is adapted from Claire Kilroy's novel, "Tenderwire", narrated in the voice of Eva Tyne, an Irish violinist living and working in New York. The story involves Alexander who has offered Eva the opportunity to buy a rare violin, a Stradivarius, at a fraction of its market value. However, this violin comes without documents of identity or rightful ownership.

Nobody believed the real story of how I found the Magdalena (all old violins have names and Magdalena is this one's name). Her origins are suspicious at best. I got her from a Russian. At least I thought he was Russian. He was a giant of a man and blond as a child. His name, he told me, was Alexander. I encountered him in a bar done up like a KGB office, or a New York bar owner's impression of one: red lights, black walls, yellow scythes. I couldn't say at what point Alexander started telling me about violins, about a very special one, about a Stradivarius.

That name was all it took and I was in the passenger seat of a battered car driving at speed over the East River to Alexander's apartment, a few blocks away. Here he produced the violin, holding it out like a cushion on which a crown is placed. "It is the real thing, I promise you," he said. By agreeing there and then to pay him 600,000 dollars, I confirmed that this violin was no ordinary instrument. As a musician you instinctively sense when something is special and I heard something special when I put bow to string and began to play. I heard something that unveiled an Aladdin's cave of possibilities.

This is not what Zach, manager of the orchestra I played in, thought, when I related the encounter to him: "The more I hear, the worse it gets," he said. "It's either fake, or worse — it's the real thing and the Russian doesn't have a rightful claim on it; it'll be seized within days of your first performance. Have you considered what that will do to your career? Being linked with a stolen violin? You might be arrested? You'll be deported from the States at least." The absoluteness of his voice, the surety of his manner: everything Zach said was right. Logical, reasonable and right. And yet I couldn't allow myself to agree with him.

When Zach left, I organised the money that I had managed to get together. Everything my father had left me and more for a violin. The cash formed an unwieldy bulk. How was I to transport it to Tompkins Square Park where I had arranged to meet Alexander? What was to stop him from grabbing it and making off? I swept the money into one large pile and made a big pyramid of it, a drift of autumn leaves, then shoved it into a plastic bag. Now it had no separate identity. It was just counters in a game. A game of high risk.

Saturday night's blizzard had deposited an icing of snow. New York has a way of seeming brand-new sometimes. I put on my runners in case I had to run and stepped out onto the street. The faces around me looked fresh in the bracing whiteness. I tried not to look in their eyes lest they detect the alarm in mine. It was natural to feel jittery as the pressure of walking around with such a large sum was breathtaking. I took out my inhaler and wheezed piteously. There was a faint warmth in the January sun that shone on my face.

I wiped snow off a bench and sat on it. My hands in my lap were like two dead puppies. Between them was the plastic bag. I was happy, that was the odd thing. It was like sitting in a darkened cinema waiting for a horror movie to begin.

Then I saw Alexander as he trudged doggedly through the snow. Shafts of sunlight spilled through the trees onto his ash-blond hair, causing it to flicker like fire. He cut through the centre of the park, sat down beside me and let out a companionable sigh as he placed the violin case by my feet. "Open it," he grinned, as if it were a carefully chosen gift.

I put the plastic bag on the ground and wedged it securely between my ankles, then lifted the lid of the case. It looked like the same violin. My hands unstrapped it, fine-tuned the strings and then hesitantly sounded the high notes. How ethereal they were on the icy air.

It was the first time since childhood that I'd played outdoors and in the frozen world of Tompkins Square Park, the sound was startlingly pure. I was almost laughing, almost crying in wonder at the loveliness of the sound. I listened to the laughter of the children in the playground, the cooing of the woodpigeons, the barking in the dog run.

If I was about to make the biggest mistake of my life, then so be it.

N.B. Candidates may NOT answer Question A and Question B on the same text.

Questions A and B carry 50 marks each.

QUESTION A

(i)   "A game of high risk!" Give **three** pieces of evidence from the text which suggest that Eva was "about to make the biggest mistake" of her life.   (15)

(ii)   What impression of the character Eva Tyne is created in this extract? Support your answer with reference to the text.   (15)

(iii)   One reviewer of the novel *Tenderwire* described it as "a compelling and well-written thriller". From your reading of the extract, do you agree with this view? Refer to the text in support of your answer.   (20)

QUESTION B

Write **two** diary entries: **one written by Alexander**, recalling his encounter with Eva in Tompkins Square Park and the **second by Zach**, giving his thoughts on hearing that Eva has purchased the violin.   (50)

TEXT 3
CLUES TO IDENTITY

This text consists of a visual and written element adapted from a series in the Guardian *newspaper entitled "Writers' rooms" where photographer Eamonn McCabe talks to writers about their places of work.*

John Banville's room

John Banville

In my time I have had to make do with some strange work-spaces. To write fiction I must have my own desk, my own wall with my own postcards pinned to it, and my own window not to look out of.

My present study – a word that always makes me uneasy, I am not sure why – is a small apartment in a huge, anonymous block in Dublin city centre. My window, the one I do not look out of, gives on to a courtyard where no one ever goes, and where the silence is day-long and almost pastoral. When I first began to come here to work, a dozen years ago, I used to shut my door on entering each morning and put the chain on. The place is clean, or cleanish, and, yes, well lighted. Here I am out of reach. Or so I like to imagine.

Nicola Barker

I've never had a study - never really needed one. I like to work in the middle of things, so my desk is in the far corner of my living-room, pressed up against the kitchen cabinets. I have a beautiful view of the river but I rarely turn to look at it. I'm very focused when I work. I wear a pair of industrial earmuffs, even though I'm partially deaf and don't really need them. I love the gushing silence they provide and the pressure of them against my head. My desk is my camp, my small launch, my treehouse. It's made from some old stairs and it has loads of little cupboards in front full of interesting stuff – letters and rosary beads, faulty discs, stickers and whatnot. As I work, my dog, Watson, insists on positioning himself under my chair which has a little arch cut into it just big enough for him to slot his head through. In general it's always possible to tell which phase I'm in with a project by the number of books piled up on my desk. At the start there's just a few, by the end they pose a serious health-and-safety hazard.

Nicola Barker's room

Russell Hoban's room

Russell Hoban

This room is composed of tottering stacks and shaky heaps of DVDs and videos, bulging shelves of books, slithery carpets of undiscarded draft pages, and delicately balanced objects of various weight and fragility poised to fall on my head. I have often been buried under DVD slides and video-topplings and once the TV fell on me while I was trying to squeeze between it and a precarious stack. Luckily the fallen DVDs I landed on acted as a shock absorber for the weight of the TV, which might have broken one or two legs otherwise. I accept daily bruises as a matter of course.

I can't always find what I'm looking for, and many of my books, although visible, are out of reach because of stacks and heaps in front of the shelves and no floor space for a ladder. In cases like this it is more economical to buy a new DVD, CD or book than to spend a day in search-and-rescue operations. This room, full of all kinds of reference materials, is almost an extension of my brain.

N.B.   Candidates may NOT answer Question A and Question B on the same text.

Questions A and B carry 50 marks each.

QUESTION A

(i)   What impression of each of the three writers' personalities do you form from the **written texts** describing their places of work?   (15)

(ii)   If you had to choose **one** of these rooms to study in, which would you select? Refer to the **image** of the chosen room in support of your answer.   (15)

(iii)   Select **<u>one</u> of the other two images** of the writers' rooms and write a detailed description of it. You might consider the use of colour, light, details or objects in the image.
[In your answer you may not re-use the image you have selected in question (ii).]   (20)

QUESTION B

Students in your school have been invited to contribute articles to the school website on issues relevant to young people. This week's issue is "**We are what we wear**". Write an article for the website expressing your views on the topic.   (50)

SECTION II
COMPOSING (100 marks)

Write a composition on **any one** of the following.

Each composition carries 100 marks.

The composition assignments below are intended to reflect language study in the areas of information, argument, persuasion, narration, and the aesthetic use of language.

1. "...advised adults to treat adolescents with sympathy, appreciation and respect..." (TEXT 1)

    Write a magazine article (serious and/or light-hearted) in which you give advice to adults on how to help teenagers cope with the "storm and stress" of adolescence.

2. "...the new global society."   (TEXT 1)

    Write a speech in which you argue for or against the necessity to protect national culture and identity.

3. "...17-year-old male protagonist with a darting gaze..."   (TEXT 1)

    Write a short story in which the central character is a rebellious teenager (male or female).

4. "I have a beautiful view..."   (TEXT 3)

    Write a personal essay in which you describe a place that you consider beautiful.

5. "...fake, or worse..."   (TEXT 2)

    Write the text of a talk you would deliver to your classmates on the topic:
    Appearances can be Deceptive.

6. "I was happy..."   (TEXT 2)

    Write an article for a school magazine in which you explore aspects of life that make you happy.

7. "...my camp, my small launch, my treehouse."   (TEXT 3)

    Write a short story in which setting/location is a significant feature.
    (Your story may be prompted by one or more of the locations depicted in Text 3 or by any other setting of your choice.)

31

Coimisiún na Scrúduithe Stáit
State Examinations Commission

LEAVING CERTIFICATE EXAMINATION, 2008

English - Higher Level - Paper 2

Total Marks: 200

Thursday, 5th June – Morning, 9.30 – 12.50

Candidates must attempt the following:-

- **ONE** question from SECTION I – The Single Text
- **ONE** question from SECTION II – The Comparative Study
- **ONE** question on the Unseen Poem from SECTION III – Poetry
- **ONE** question on Prescribed Poetry from SECTION III – Poetry

N.B. Candidates must answer on Shakespearean Drama.
They may do so in SECTION I, The Single Text (*Othello*) or in SECTION II, The Comparative Study (*Othello, Hamlet, As You Like It*).

INDEX OF SINGLE TEXTS

SECTION I

THE SINGLE TEXT (60 marks)

Candidates must answer **one** question from this section (A – E).

A WUTHERING HEIGHTS – Emily Brontë

(i) "Although his passion for revenge horrifies us, Heathcliff still remains the most appealing character in the novel *Wuthering Heights*."

Discuss this statement supporting your answer with the aid of suitable reference to the text.

OR

(ii) "In reading *Wuthering Heights* powerful imagery and symbolism contribute to our appreciation of the novel."

Discuss this statement supporting your answer with the aid of suitable reference to the text.

B THE REMAINS OF THE DAY – Kazuo Ishiguro

(i) "I can't even say I made my own mistakes....what dignity is there in that?"

(Mr Stevens)

Write your personal assessment of the character of Stevens in the light of this quotation. Support your answer with the aid of suitable reference to the text.

OR

(ii) "The novel *The Remains of the Day* offers the reader a fascinating insight into the lives of the wealthy and the ordinary people in the England of the 1930s."

Discuss this statement with the aid of suitable reference to the text.

C   DEATH AND NIGHTINGALES – Eugene McCabe

(i)   "How extraordinarily beautiful the world could be and all the creatures in it, excepting mankind."

Write a personal response to the world of *Death and Nightingales* in the light of this quotation from the novel. Support your answer with the aid of suitable reference to the text.

OR

(ii)   "Beth Winters is the heroine of the novel *Death and Nightingales.*"

Do you agree with this statement? Support your answer with the aid of suitable reference to the text.

D   THE CRUCIBLE – Arthur Miller

(i)   " …a person is either with this court or he must be counted against it."

Where do your sympathies lie in the conflict between Judge Danforth and John Proctor?

Support your answer with the aid of suitable reference to the text.

OR

(ii)   Compare and contrast the characters of Elizabeth Proctor and Abigail Williams, supporting your answer with the aid of suitable reference to the text.

E   OTHELLO – William Shakespeare

(i)   "Othello's foolishness rather than Iago's cleverness leads to the tragedy of Shakespeare's *Othello*."

Discuss this statement supporting your answer with the aid of suitable reference to the text.

OR

(ii)   "Shakespeare's play *Othello* demonstrates the weakness of human judgement."

Discuss this statement supporting your answer with the aid of suitable reference to the text.

SECTION II

THE COMPARATIVE STUDY (70 marks)

Candidates must answer **one** question from **either A** – Theme or Issue
or B – Literary Genre.

In your answer you may not use the text you have answered on in **SECTION I** – The Single
Text.

N.B. The questions use the word **text** to refer to all the different kinds of texts available for
study on this course, i.e. novel, play, short story, autobiography, biography, travel writing, and
film. The questions use the word **author** to refer to novelists, playwrights, writers in all genres,
and film-directors.

A   THEME OR ISSUE

1. "The comparative study of a theme or issue allows the reader/viewer to gain a
    variety of viewpoints on that theme or issue."

    (a)   Describe the viewpoint on your chosen theme or issue that emerges from
           one of your comparative texts.   (30)

    (b)   Compare the viewpoints on the same theme in the **other two texts** that you
           have studied.   (40)

OR

2. "There are key moments in a text when a theme comes sharply into focus."

    Compare how key moments from the texts you have studied brought a theme or
    issue into sharp focus.   (70)

B   LITERARY GENRE

1.   "A good text will have moments of great emotional power."

   (a)   With reference to a key moment in **one** of your texts show how this
         emotional power was created.   (30)

   (b)   Take key moments from the **other two texts** from your comparative course
         and compare the way in which the emotional power of these scenes was
         created.   (40)

                                        OR

2.   "The creation of memorable characters is part of the art of good story-telling."

      Write an essay comparing the ways in which memorable characters were
      created and contributed to your enjoyment of the stories in the texts you have
      studied for your comparative course. It will be sufficient to refer to the creation
      of **one** character from each of your chosen texts.   (70)

SECTION III

POETRY (70 marks)

Candidates must answer **A** – Unseen Poem **and B** – Prescribed Poetry.

A   UNSEEN POEM (20 marks)

Answer **either** Question **1** or Question **2**.

Those Winter Sundays

Sundays too my father got up early
and put his clothes on in the blueblack cold,
then with cracked hands that ached
from labour in the weekday weather made
banked fires blaze. No one ever thanked him.

 I'd wake and hear the cold splintering, breaking.
When the rooms were warm, he'd call,
and slowly I would rise and dress,
fearing the chronic angers of that house,

Speaking indifferently to him,
who had driven out the cold
and polished my good shoes as well.
What did I know, what did I know
of love's austere[1] and lonely offices[2]?

Robert Hayden

1. austere: harsh, strict

2. office: duty, service, daily worship

1.   (a)   What impression of the father-son relationship do you get from this poem?   (10)

     (b)   Choose a phrase or line from the poem that impressed you.
            Explain your choice.   (10)

OR

2.   Write a personal response to this poem. Your answer should make close
      reference to the text.   (20)

B   PRESCRIBED POETRY (50 marks)

Candidates must answer **one** of the following questions (**1 – 4**).

1.   Philip Larkin

"Writing about unhappiness is the source of my popularity." (Philip Larkin)

In the light of Larkin's own assessment of his popularity, write an essay outlining your reasons for liking/not liking his poetry. Support your points with the aid of suitable reference to the poems you have studied.

2.   John Donne

"John Donne uses startling imagery and wit in his exploration of relationships."

Give your response to the poetry of John Donne in the light of this statement. Support your points with the aid of suitable reference to the poems you have studied.

3.   Derek Mahon

"Derek Mahon explores people and places in his own distinctive style."

Write your response to this statement supporting your points with the aid of suitable reference to the poems you have studied.

4.   Adrienne Rich

"the desire to be heard, - that is the impulse behind writing poems, for me."
                                                                    (Adrienne Rich)

Does the poetry of Adrienne Rich speak to you? Write your personal response, referring to the poems of Adrienne Rich that do/do not speak to you.

38

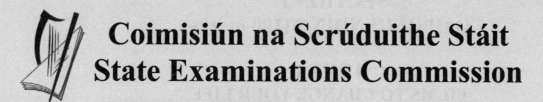

Coimisiún na Scrúduithe Stáit
State Examinations Commission

LEAVING CERTIFICATE EXAMINATION, 2007

English – Higher Level – Paper I

Total Marks: 200

Wednesday, 6th June – Morning, 9.30 – 12.20

- This paper is divided into two sections,
  Section I COMPREHENDING and Section II COMPOSING.
- The paper contains **three** texts on the general theme of CHANGE.
- Candidates should familiarise themselves with each of the texts before beginning their answers.

- Both sections of this paper (COMPREHENDING and COMPOSING) must be attempted.
- Each section carries 100 marks.

SECTION I – COMPREHENDING

- Two Questions, A and B, follow each text.
- Candidates must answer a Question A on one text and a Question B on a different text. Candidates must answer only one Question A and only one Question B.
- **N.B.** Candidates may NOT answer a Question A and a Question B on the same text.

SECTION II – COMPOSING

- Candidates must write on **one** of the compositions 1 – 7.

SECTION I
COMPREHENDING (100 marks)

TEXT 1
FILMS TO CHANGE YOUR LIFE

The following text is based on extracts from the recent publication, "1000 Films to Change your Life", edited by Simon Cropper.

I never went to the cinema as a child. As a bookish teenager I loved reading and going to the theatre. I felt film could not rival the blood-and-sweat physicality of live drama. It seemed impossible that film could ever give voice to the idealism and tangled passions that raged in my teenage heart.

And then, luckily, I happened to see Vittorio De Sica's "Bicycle Thieves". A simple story at heart, it charts the struggles of proud but unemployed father, Antonio Ricci, to find a job in post-war Italy that will let him feed his wife and child. He is finally offered work – pasting film posters across the city – but he has to lie and pretend he has a bicycle. His wife pawns their bed sheets so he can get one, but it is stolen almost immediately. For the rest of the film he wanders up and down the city, often with his young son in tow, trying to track down the thief. The anger he reveals, both in the words that he yells as well as in every eloquent close-up of his

face, underlines his frustration. Ricci's defiance demonstrates that this is not the way society should be. That simple idea is the first and most important stage in encouraging viewers to imagine what a better society would look like.

Documentaries can achieve the same effect. Among the most well known are those of journalist-turned-film-maker Michael Moore. Whether taking on the chairman of General Motors in "Roger and Me", the powerful gun industry in "Bowling for Columbine", or the Bush administration in "Fahrenheit 9/11", he concocts an old-fashioned tale of good versus evil and casts himself as the underdog yapping away at the heels of political and corporate giants.

Political films also set out to make us see the world in a new and clearer light. Without explicit commentary they dramatise issues like the oil-industry drama, "Syriana", or "Erin Brokovich" the true story of a single mother's exposé of an industry water poisoning case. These films make an impact because you reflect on the issues raised and this strengthens your own views and understanding.

But cinema doesn't just make us think. It makes us laugh too. Humour is impossible to define but it's about something that's in us all. It's about the mistakes we make and the craziness of the world we live in. Ben Stiller's fashion spoof, "Zoolander", is a wonderful satire on the vanity and corruption of the fashion industry. Comedy has always been best at mocking pretensions and can say quite as much as drama and documentary while reaching a bigger audience. Group laughter in a darkened movie-theatre is also a comforting, confidence-building mode of social bonding.

Then there are, of course, the great positive movie moments that can and do take you out of yourself, lift your mood, crack a smile, raise your spirits. Classic Hollywood films continue to exert a glamorous spell over our imaginations. Taking the regular television schedules as an indicator of our taste in cinema, we see "The Wizard of Oz", "It's a Wonderful Life", "The Sound of Music", to name only the most obvious titles. All underline our need for the guaranteed joy that these endlessly repeatable movies provide.

Nothing entertains us like the movies but they also have the power to ignite strong passions. A film can make us laugh, make us sad, frighten or reassure us, make us angry – and even sometimes make us want to change the world.

N.B. **Candidates may NOT answer Question A and Question B on the same text.**

Questions A and B carry 50 marks each.

QUESTION A

(i) In what way, according to the author of this text, do films change the way we think and/or feel about life? Support your answer by reference to the text.

(15)

(ii) As a teenager the writer found reading books more rewarding and appealing than watching films. Has this been your experience? Explain your answer.

(15)

(iii) What features of the writer's style help to make this an interesting piece to read? Support your answer by reference to the text. (20)

QUESTION B

Imagine you are running for the position of Student Council President in your school. Compose an informative election leaflet encouraging students to vote for you. It should outline your own leadership qualities and the changes you would like to introduce into your school. (50)

TEXT 2

LONDON, PAST AND PRESENT

In 1930, wandering through London for a series of magazine articles, Virginia Woolf found a city alive with bustling activity and excitement. Here, novelist Monica Ali takes a 21st century stroll in Woolf's footsteps – and seventy-five years later finds London humming to a different tune.

Piccadilly circus, early 1900s   Piccadilly circus today

Following in Virginia Woolf's footsteps, I begin at the Thames on a hot, cloudless day. I sit on a bench and read from her article about the city of London in 1930:

"As we come closer to the Tower Bridge the domes swell and church spires, white with age, mingle with the tapering, pencil-shaped chimneys of factories".

I look at the London before me today and see no factory chimneys. The spires and domes are overshadowed by the glass towers, smoky, clear and pallid green. Red buses splash across London Bridge. Cranes, one white, one blue, make their majestic swings at distant building sites. Only the river refuses to sparkle in the sun. It is resolutely, doggedly brown.

The hustle and bustle of the docks described by Woolf –

"the ships lying captive beneath the warehouses, the hoisting of barrels, sacks and crates, the lorries jostling in the narrow lanes to shift the wool that the cart horses struggle to distribute"

– have vanished. The immense, plain and unornamented warehouses through which

Woolf meandered so many years ago, nowadays contain a mix of luxury apartments, offices, restaurants and shops. Air-conditioning units chant and hum but there is no *"roar"* here now. I wonder at this new, noiseless commerce, at how it works unseen and wrapped around in shrouds of glass.

I tune in to conversations around me. Office workers hold meetings in the open-air with cappuccinos and almond-laden croissants. "Spreadsheet" I hear, and "gameplan" and "yeah we should talk about that sometime". These fake meetings with folders offered like excuses reflect today's world of mighty commerce.

Modern London is a thirsty, ravenous city, ready at every moment to eat and drink. Woolf passed from east to west of the city without giving meals a thought, but today, at every step, we are encouraged to sit down at once and eat. I wander up and down, counting cafés and restaurants: Chop House, Pizza Express, Starbucks, cafés without names. For all that it is chic and smart there is something dispiriting about these cobbled streets. I do not like this Starbucks world. And yet what romance existed in the old cloth-capped world of 1930 where dockers waited at warehouse gates in hope of work?

I join other tourists queuing for the "Tower Bridge Experience" – a series of audio-visual presentations, with robotic characters to guide you through the story of this world-famous London landmark. It saves you the bother of imagining, by providing special effects, including sounds and smells. I am dispirited again and not because I mourn for a lost London but because it is so difficult to see the London that is there for myself. We must now buy "The Experience".

Woolf turned her attention to churches and now I too seek out St Paul's Cathedral. Here we are invited first of all to contemplate, not God, but our stomachs. Before you can skip up the steps to the broad porch, you stumble over a sandwich board announcing "The Place Below", the café that is installed in the crypt. The cathedral no longer dominates the London skyline as it did in the past but it still retains the *"splendour" and "architectural grandeur"* of which Woolf wrote. It is the sense of mystery and serenity that is missing. We are greeted by a voice which speaks in warm and friendly tones, the kind of customer-centred "care" that we have come to expect. "St Paul's audio tour. Try me! Thank you for visiting us. We hope that you leave the cathedral inspired and refreshed".

When Woolf passed through what she described as *"the excitement and gaudiness"* of Oxford Street, she saw shopkeepers competing vigorously to meet the needs and desires of customers with *"windows lit up by night and banners flaunting by day"*. Now as I stand here I realize there is still a liveliness that will not be tamed. The discount stores brag of bargains; the souvenir shops are proudly tacky; the smell of fast food is everywhere and the music unapologetically loud. London is truly here, in all its ethnic mix. Despite the push-and-pull of commerce the heart of this place is unchanged.

N.B. **Candidates may NOT answer Question A and Question B on the same text.**

Questions A and B carry 50 marks each.

QUESTION A

(i) Virginia Woolf described London in 1930 as a *"city alive"*. In your own words, outline the aspects of the city that impressed her most. (15)

(ii) Monica Ali uses a number of vivid images to portray the modern city of London. Select **three** that you consider particularly effective and explain why. (15)

(iii) If given the choice, in which of the two Londons, (the one described by Virginia Woolf in 1930 or the modern city experienced by Monica Ali) would you choose to live? Give reasons for your choice with reference to the text. (20)

QUESTION B

Imagine your local radio station is producing a series of programmes entitled "Changing Times", in which teenagers are asked to give their views on **the changes they welcome** in the world around them. You have been invited to contribute. Write out the text of the presentation you would make.

(50)

TEXT 3
FORCES FOR CHANGE?

❶ The Ballot Box

❷ War

❸ Natural Disaster

❻ Protest

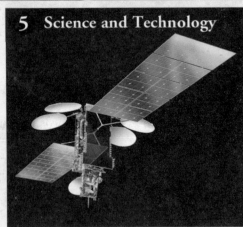

❺ Science and Technology

❹ The Smoking Ban

N.B. Candidates may **NOT** answer Question A and Question B on the same text.

Questions A and B carry 50 marks each.

QUESTION A

(i)   Select **one** of the visual images in this collection for the front cover of a book entitled "Forces for Change in our World". Give reasons why you consider your chosen image to be the most effective and/or suitable.   (15)

(ii)   Does this set of images represent a balanced view of our changing world? Support your view by reference to the images.   (15)

(iii) If asked to select another image to expand this group of images depicting forces for change, what image would you suggest? Give reasons for your choice.   (20)

QUESTION B

Imagine you have a friend in another country which is considering the introduction of a ban on smoking in public places.
Write a letter to your friend advising him/her **either** to support **or** not to support the proposed ban.
In giving your advice you may wish to draw on the recent experience of the smoking ban in Ireland.
                                        (50)

SECTION II
COMPOSING (100 marks)

Write a composition on **any one** of the following.

Each composition carries 100 marks.

The composition assignments below are intended to reflect language study in the areas of information, argument, persuasion, narration, and the aesthetic use of language.

1. "… the idealism and tangled passions that raged in my teenage heart."

   (TEXT 1)

   Write a personal essay on the idealism and passions of youth.

2. "And yet what romance existed in the old cloth-capped world …"

   (TEXT 2)

   Write a speech in which you attempt to persuade an audience that the past should not be glorified.

3. "I tune in to conversations around me."   (TEXT 2)

   Write a short story suggested by the above sentence.

4. "…the needs and desires of customers…"   (TEXT 2)

   Write a magazine article (serious or light-hearted) entitled: "The Modern Shopping Centre".

5. "…make us want to change the world."   (TEXT 1)

   Write the text of a talk, serious or humorous, to be given to your peers, entitled: "How I intend to change the world!"

6. "…the first and most important stage in encouraging viewers to imagine…"

   (TEXT 1)

   Write an article for a popular magazine on the importance of the imagination.

7. **Write a short story prompted by one or more of the images in TEXT 3.**

Coimisiún na Scrúduithe Stáit
State Examinations Commission

LEADING CERTIFICATE EXAMINATION, 2007

English - Higher Level - Paper 2

Total Marks: 200

Wednesday, 6 June – Afternoon, 1.30 – 4.50

Candidates must attempt the following:-

- **ONE** question from SECTION I – The Single Text
- **ONE** question from SECTION II – The Comparative Study
- **ONE** question on the Unseen Poem from SECTION III – Poetry
- **ONE** question on Prescribed Poetry from SECTION III – Poetry

N.B. Candidates must answer on Shakespearean Drama.

They may do so in SECTION I, The Single Text (*Macbeth*) or in SECTION II, The Comparative Study (*Macbeth, Twelfth Night, As You Like It*).

SECTION I

THE SINGLE TEXT (60 marks)

Candidates must answer **one** question from this section (A – E).

A   **PRIDE AND PREJUDICE** – Jane Austen

(i)   Jane Austen particularly liked Elizabeth Bennet as a character. Did you?

Write your personal response to the character of Elizabeth outlining the qualities that did or did not appeal to you. Your answer should make use of reference to the text in support of your points.

OR

(ii)   "Marriage rather than love is the central theme of *Pride and Prejudice*."

Do you agree with this assessment of the novel? Give reasons for your answer supporting them with the aid of suitable reference to the text.

B   **WUTHERING HEIGHTS** – Emily Brontë

(i)   "In *Wuthering Heights*, Emily Brontë introduces us to a strange and supernatural world."

Does she succeed in making this strange and supernatural world believable? Explain your answer, supporting your point of view with suitable reference to the text.

OR

(ii)   "We admire the younger Catherine (Linton) because she is so different from her mother (Cathy Earnshaw)."

Do you agree with this statement? Make an argument in support of your point of view with the aid of suitable reference to the text.

C   THE POISONWOOD BIBLE – Barbara Kingsolver

(i)   *"Adah and I were trying to puzzle out how everything you thought you knew means something different in Africa."*

Write a personal response to the world of Africa that you experienced as a reader of *The Poisonwood Bible*. Support your answer with the aid of suitable reference to the text.

OR

(ii)   *"You can't just sashay into the jungle aiming to change it all over to the Christian style, without expecting the jungle to change you right back."*

Discuss the way in which **any two** of the Price family were or were not changed as a result of their experiences in the Congo. Support your answer with the aid of suitable reference to the text.

D   DEATH OF A SALESMAN – Arthur Miller

(i)   "Willy Loman is not a likeable character, but he attracts our sympathy."

Write a response to this statement. Support your answer with the aid of suitable reference to the text.

OR

(ii)   Write the text of a talk that you would give to your class outlining the reasons why the play *Death of a Salesman* is worth reading. Your talk should include detailed reference to the play.

E   MACBETH – William Shakespeare

(i)   "The relationship between Macbeth and Lady Macbeth undergoes significant change during the course of the play."

Discuss this statement supporting your answer with the aid of suitable reference to the text.

OR

(ii)   "Essentially the play *Macbeth* is about power, its use and abuse."

Discuss this view of the play, supporting your answer with the aid of suitable reference to the text.

SECTION II

THE COMPARATIVE STUDY (70 marks)

Candidates must answer **one** question from **either A** – The General Vision and Viewpoint **or B** – The Cultural Context.

In your answer you may not use the text you have answered on in **SECTION I** – The Single Text.

N.B. The questions use the word **text** to refer to all the different kinds of texts available for study on this course, i.e. novel, play, short story, autobiography, biography, travel writing, and film. The questions use the word **author** to refer to novelists, playwrights, writers in all genres, and film-directors.

A   THE GENERAL VISION AND VIEWPOINT

1. "A reader's understanding of the general vision and viewpoint is influenced by key moments in the text."

    (a)   Choose a key moment from one of your chosen texts and show how it influenced your understanding of the general vision and viewpoint.

    (30)

    (b)   With reference to two other chosen texts compare the way in which key moments influence your understanding of the general vision and viewpoint of those texts.

    (40)

    OR

2. " The general vision and viewpoint is shaped by the reader's feeling of optimism or pessimism in reading the text."

    In the light of the above statement, compare the general vision and viewpoint in **at least two texts** you have studied in your comparative course.   (70)

B   THE CULTURAL CONTEXT

1. Imagine that you are a journalist sent to investigate the cultural context of
    the worlds of the three texts from your comparative course.

    (a) Write an article on the cultural context that you found most interesting. (30)

    (b) In a second article compare the cultural contexts of the other two worlds
        with each other.   (40)

OR

2. "The cultural context can have a significant influence on the behaviour
    of the central character/characters in a text."

    Compare the way in which the behaviour of the central characters in **at least
    two** of our texts is influenced b   the cultural context of those texts.
                                                                                 (70)

SECTION III
POETRY (70 marks)

Candidates must answer **A** – Unseen Poem **and B** – Prescribed Poetry.

A   **UNSEEN POEM** (20 marks)

Answer **either** Question **1 or** Question **2**.

(Ben Ziman-Bright is a young poet from London. He won the Young Poets on the Underground Competition in 2004 with this poem. It was displayed on the London Underground.)

Rhapsody

Sat in the cheap seats
Of Symphony Hall, squinting
As the instruments tuned up,
I could pick out only you:
Fourth row back and clutching
Your viola, bright hair spilt
Across the strings. You were
Deep in a flurry of pages
With bitten lip, too
Intent on forcing that
Melody right to the cheap seats
To notice me up there, ears straining
To block out any sound but yours.

Ben Ziman-Bright

1.   Describe the impact that this poem makes on you as a reader.   (20)

OR

2.   Discuss the ways in which this poem captures the emotions felt by the poet.   (20)

B PRESCRIBED POETRY (50 marks)

Candidates must answer **one** of the following questions (**1 – 4**).

1. **"Robert Frost – a poet of sadness?"**

   Write an introduction to the poetry of Robert Frost using the above title.

   Your introduction should address his themes and the impact of his poetry on you as a reader. Support your points with reference to the poems you have studied.

2. **The Poetry of T.S. Eliot – a personal journey.**

   Write a personal response to the poems by T.S. Eliot on your course. Support your points with reference to the poetry on your course.

3. **The Impact of John Montague's Poetry**

   Write a speech to be delivered to your classmates on the impact that John Montague's poetry had on you. Your answer should focus on both themes and the use of imagery/language. Support your points with the aid of suitable reference to the poems on your course.

4. **"The poetry of Sylvia Plath is intense, deeply personal, and quite disturbing."**

   Do you agree with this assessment of her poetry? Write a response, supporting your points with the aid of suitable reference to the poems you have studied.

Coimisiún na Scrúduithe Stáit
State Examinations Commission

LEAVING CERTIFICATE EXAMINATION, 2006

English – Higher Level – Paper I

Total Marks: 200

Wednesday, 7 June – Morning, 9.30 – 12.20

- This paper is divided into two sections,
  Section I COMPREHENDING and Section II COMPOSING.
- The paper contains **three** texts on the general theme of PRETENCE.
- Candidates should familiarise themselves with each of the texts before beginning their answers.

- Both sections of this paper (COMPREHENDING and COMPOSING) must be attempted.
- Each section carries 100 marks.

SECTION I – COMPREHENDING

- Two Questions, A and B, follow each text.
- Candidates must answer a Question A on one text and a Question B on a different text. Candidates must answer only one Question A and only one Question B.
- **N.B.** Candidates may NOT answer a Question A and a Question B on the same text.

SECTION II – COMPOSING

- Candidates must write on **one** of the compositions 1 – 7.

SECTION I
COMPREHENDING (100 Marks)

TEXT I
"WHAT SEEMS TO BE THE PROBLEM, LADY SARAH?"

In this extract (adapted from **A Border Station,** *by Shane Connaughton) a father and son are cutting down a tree. The father, a garda sergeant, has been given permission by Lady Sarah, a member of the landed gentry, to cut down a small tree on her lands. However, he decides to ignore her wishes and cut down a magnificent beech tree on the avenue leading to the Great House. We join the story as the tree falls…*

"She's going," said his father. Branches quaking, the huge tree tilted, twisted and, fighting to stay upright, grabbed at a neighbouring tree but, bowing to its fate, keeled over and with a creaking goodbye-sigh rushed to the earth with a thunderous hurricane crash. The boy felt the shock waves in his feet and saw the light flood in to the space where the tree had stood. It was mad, he thought. Ridiculous. Lady Sarah was bound to find out. His father grinned.

"It'll see us in firewood for the winter, thank God."

Tired out he sat on the tree-stump beside his father and had alternate swigs at the bottle of cold tea.

Hearing a noise he turned his head and instantly his body and blood went cold. Approaching along at the wheel of her antiquated Rolls Royce was Lady Sarah. Time stopped dead. His father gave a strangled groan and his face iced over in hatred. They were caught like rats in a trap.

The car crunched to a halt. He was terrified in case his father did something desperate and was all the more amazed when he saw him smiling and in high good nature waving to Lady Sarah as she, horror-stricken, stepped onto the drive. Wearing a peculiar 1920s hat and a flapping plastic mack she dismissed his father's greeting and staggered towards the tree.

"What have you done, Sergeant, what have you done!" she wailed. "You have killed one of my beauties!"

Grabbing and clutching the stricken branches she buried herself in the copper coloured leaves.

"Oh Beatrice, Beatrice, my beauty, how has this occurred?"

His father winked.

"What's wrong, what seems to be the problem, Lady Sarah?"

"The problem," she replied, stepping from the tree, "is that you have murdered the wrong tree." Behind the thick lenses of her spectacles her eyes were tiny red dots of dismay.

"Oh no, we haven't, have we?" howled his father, his face a dancing mask of pantomime surprise. "Good Lord, I can't believe it. Are you sure Lady Sarah?"

"Oh yes I'm sure alright. I gave you a weakling ash, not this!"

Suddenly he turned on the boy and made as if to strike him.

"Didn't I tell you it wasn't this one? I told you all along."

The boy hung his head in shame and didn't dare look at Lady Sarah because he knew she knew his father lied.

"I'll do anything I can by way of reparation, anything. I remember you saying the tree's name is Andy. I think that's what confused me. That and the boy. Beech wood is no good to me anyway. It's a poor burner. A weakling ash is just what I wanted, Lady Sarah."

Once more he blamed the boy and made a run at him as if to hit him. Darting out of his way he went close to Lady Sarah and looked into her eyes.

She knew.
Turning away she faced the dead Beatrice and with her frail hand plucked a copper leaf.
Resting on her fingers like a clot of blood, she held it to her mouth and nose and sighed as if kissing goodbye to a loved one. Tears welled in the boy's eyes. Lady Sarah looked very old, very sad, and a little frightened. She owned the great demesne, employed many people, but up against his father she knew the truth. He was the Garda Sergeant and she was just a lonely spinster, powerless to command. She needed him to protect her property. The law was hers but it was on his word that it was carried out.
Getting into her car, she spoke softly, her pride hurt, her spirit shocked.
"You may as well finish what you so cruelly started."
"Well that's the only damn thing we can do now, Lady Sarah."
Hours later as they drove home, though his body ached, the boy's soul raged rampant at the conquering smirk on his father's face.

N.B.   Candidates may NOT answer Question A and Question B on the same text.

Questions A and B carry 50 marks each.

QUESTION A

(i)   Do you consider the first paragraph to be an example of good descriptive writing? Explain your view.   (15)

(ii)   How do the boy's feelings towards Lady Sarah change as the narrative progresses? Support your answer by reference to the text.   (15)

(iii)   A reader of the passage has commented: "Both Lady Sarah and the father are powerful, but in different ways."
What, in your opinion, would have led the reader to this conclusion?   (20)

QUESTION B

"Hours later...the boy's soul raged..."

Imagine that, in an attempt to control his feelings, the boy writes into his diary an account of the incident and his reactions to it.
Write out his diary entry.   (50)

TEXT 2
GHOST WRITING

Jan Stevens is a ghost writer; that is, someone who writes books that are published as the work of someone else.

On Ghost Writing

I am a ghost writer. I write books that other people take credit for – people more famous than me, or busier, or who simply can't be trusted with a pen.

I have written for well-known authors, celebrities, and even for other ghost writers who found themselves over-worked. I have written legal thrillers, historical non-fiction, mysteries, and even ghost stories. However, my name doesn't appear on the covers of any of these books, or on their copyright page. My anonymity is complete. Sometimes, even the publishers don't know I exist. My name, of course, does appear on my contracts. To prevent confusion, the language of these contracts calls me the *ghost writer* and the other party is referred to as the *author*. Under the terms of my contracts, I'm forbidden from revealing the identity of my authors. Ghost writers have to keep their secrets, or face lawsuits.

Ghost writing can be challenging. For one thing, ghost writers have to write very quickly. We are often given work that has a looming deadline. I once wrote a 120,000-word novel in twelve weeks. That's 2,000 words every day for five days a week. Maintaining this sprinter's pace at marathon length was painful, requiring much solitude and coffee. However, I made my 2,000-word count every single day without fail. One of the advantages of ghost writing is that the *almost* right word will serve as well as the *right* word.

Some ghost writers I know are haunted by the loss of recognition and go to great lengths to put secret codes into their ghost novels. They concoct sentence-length acronyms or give minor characters anagrams of their own names, so that future historians will decipher the work's true author. Others enjoy private jokes: inserting the names of cats, roommates, or favourite restaurants into their ghosted books as a kind of petty claim to ownership.

A common question asked of ghost writers is, "So, what do the *authors* actually do?" The answer covers a considerable range. I once wrote a novel from a fifty-page outline that provided specific adjectives and images for each chapter. Other authors provide only a paragraph or two. Some offer little guidance, but attack the finished work in minute detail. This ghost writer cares little because, by then, I'm busy haunting somewhere else.

As a rule, the most "prolific" authors are the most detached. I've written five books for one man whom I've never met or spoken to, or even e-mailed. His editors, however, assure me that he has actually *read* the books, and that he rather enjoyed them.

A good ghost writer is expected to pick up an author's style by reading the author's other books. I often wonder if these were, in fact, written by yet another ghost writer. Am I a copy of a copy?

So, what of the ethics of ghost writing? Is ghost writing a case of false advertising? Is it simply bad manners? It can be argued that a book is simply a product; you either enjoy it or you don't, and the author's name is no more a personal signature than the Nike logo or any other well-known trademark. Moreover, publishing is a business like any other. As in every business in a market economy, the aim is to make profit from someone else's labour. I don't object to this. Indeed, someday I hope to come up with a get-rich idea, a detective or adventure series that will be hugely successful with the reading public. I'll write the first few books in the series, and then let some other poor ghost writer follow *my* instructions for a while.

After all, I've got to know quite a few ghost writers in the last decade. Between us, I could author twenty books a year without too much effort. Indeed, when I mentioned I was going to write this essay, one of them volunteered to write it for me!

(And how do you know she didn't?)

N.B. Candidates may NOT answer Question A and Question B on the same text.

Questions A and B carry 50 marks each.

QUESTION A

(i)   On the evidence of this passage, what is the attitude of Jan Stevens to ghost writing?

(15)

(ii)   In your view, what is lost **and** gained by the '*author*' in a ghost writing arrangement? Support your answer by reference to the text. (15)

(iii)   Jan Stevens sets out to inform the reader on the topic of ghost writing. What features make this an interesting piece of informative writing? (20)

QUESTION B

Write a letter to a famous writer **or** celebrity **or** sports personality of your choice offering your services as a ghost writer for a future book. In your letter you should outline the reasons why you believe you would make a successful *ghost writer* for your chosen *author*.

(50)

TEXT 3
PRETENCE

The following text consists of a visual and a written element.

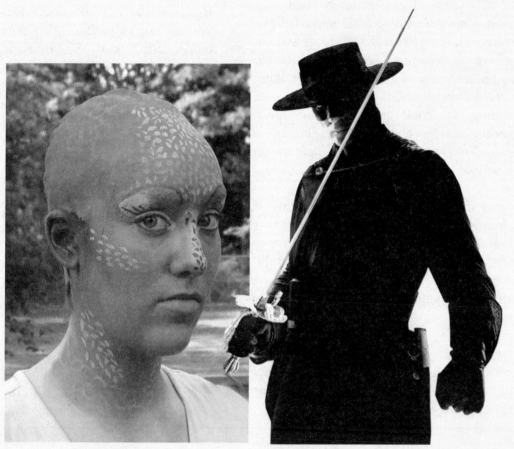

Masters of pretence

Diving?!

Make-believe

PRETENCE – Everybody's doing it!

Psychologists tell us that the habit of pretending is unique to the human species and begins in very early childhood. From about two years of age children engage in imaginary conversations with make-believe characters (talking to a doll, inventing an imaginary companion) or pretending to engage in a variety of adult activities (talking into a banana as if it were a telephone, pretending to cook and eat mud pies, pretending to be a teacher, a soldier, a Garda). The young of no other creature on earth behave like this.

It seems that this childhood role-playing is just training for later life where pretence is widespread. From the actor on stage shedding tears as he plays a tragic role for the hundredth time, to Ronaldo diving in the penalty area (again!), we are the masters of pretence.

Indeed, pretence often soothes the friction between people and promotes smoother relationships. Without it our world would be a crueller place.

Can you imagine if everyone said, "Let's stop all this pretence! Let's tell each other the unvarnished truth for a change!"

Imagine it's St. Valentine's Day and the young not so gallant lover comes to his tender lady's door. She twirls in her new dress and utters the invitation to praise. "Well? How do I look?" And he replies truthfully, "Well, let me see, dear. Hm… You know… I'd prefer you in something else!" In this case the absence of pretence might lead to a shorter than expected lifespan!

So why do we have this fascination with pretence?

Well, it is an expression of the two great gifts which make human beings unique: the gift of imagination and the ability to make one another happy.

N.B. Candidates may NOT answer Question A and Question B on the same text.

Questions A and B carry 50 marks each.

QUESTION A

(i)   In your opinion which of the visual images best expresses the theme of pretence? Explain your choice.   (15)

(ii)   Taking the images as a group, do you think they go well with the written passage? Explain your answer.   (15)

(iii) Do you think the writer is justified in the conclusions drawn in the final paragraph? Explain your view.   (20)

QUESTION B

Advertising and young people – You report to the Advertising Standards Authority.

There is much discussion as to whether or not young people are being exploited by advertisers. Write a short report to the Advertising Standards Authority outlining your views on the matter.

(50)

SECTION II
COMPOSING (100 marks)

Write a composition on **any one** of the following.

Each composition carries 100 marks.

The composition assignments below are intended to reflect language study in the areas of information, argument, persuasion, narration and the aesthetic use of language.

1. "Let's stop all this pretence! Let's tell each other the unvarnished truth for a change!"
   (TEXT 3)

   Write a personal essay in response to the above statement.

2. "Maintaining this sprinter's pace at marathon length was painful..." (TEXT 2)

   Write an article for a magazine for young adult readers in which you give them advice about how to cope with the pressures of modern living.

3. "It was mad...Ridiculous."   (TEXT 1)

   Write a short story suggested by the above title.

4. "...Someday I hope to come up with a get-rich idea..."   (TEXT 2)

   Write a magazine article (serious or light-hearted) in which you outline a get-rich idea of your own.

5. "What seems to be the problem...?"   (TEXT 1)

   Write the speech you would deliver to a group of world leaders in which you persuade them to deal with one or more of the world's problems.

6. "Imagine it's St. Valentine's Day..."   (TEXT 3)

   Write an article for a popular magazine on the importance of romance in our lives.

7. **Write a short story prompted by one or more of the images in TEXT 3.**

Coimisiún na Scrúduithe Stáit
State Examinations Commission

LEAVING CERTIFICATE EXAMINATION, 2006

English - Higher Level - Paper 2

Total Marks: 200

Wednesday, 7 June – Afternoon, 1.30 – 4.50

Candidates must attempt the following:-

- **ONE** question from SECTION I – The Single Text
- **ONE** question from SECTION II – The Comparative Study
- **ONE** question on the Unseen Poem from SECTION III – Poetry
- **ONE** question on Prescribed Poetry from SECTION III – Poetry

N.B. Candidates must answer on Shakespearean Drama.

They may do so in SECTION I, The Single Text (*King Lear, As You Like It*)

or in SECTION II, The Comparative Study (*King Lear, As You Like It, Twelfth Night*)

SECTION I

THE SINGLE TEXT (60 marks)

Candidates must answer **one** question from this section (**A – E**).

A   **PRIDE AND PREJUDICE** – Jane Austen

    (i)   "What fascinates the reader of *Pride and Prejudice* is the relationship between the central characters of Elizabeth and Mr Darcy."

            Write a response to this statement, supporting your views by reference to the text.

OR

    (ii)   "In *Pride and Prejudice* Jane Austen laughs at the follies of her characters without being cruel to them."

            To what extent would you agree with this view? Support your points by reference to the text.

B   **THE POISONWOOD BIBLE** – Barbara Kingsolver

    (i)   "The main interest in *The Poisonwood Bible* lies in the Price family's experiences of a strange and different world."

            To what extent would you agree with this view? Support your answer by reference to the text.

OR

    (ii)   Write out the text of a talk you would give in answer to the question: "Why read *The Poisonwood Bible*?" Support the points you make by reference to the novel.

C   **DEATH AND NIGHTINGALES** – Eugene McCabe

    (i)   "Violence and deception govern the relationships in *Death and Nightingales*."

            To what extent would you agree with this view? Support your answer by reference to the novel.

OR

    (ii)   "The mood or atmosphere of *Death and Nightingales* is a bleak one."

            Write a response to this statement, supporting your views by reference to the text.

D   **AS YOU LIKE IT** – William Shakespeare

(i)   What features of the drama, *As You Like It*, did you enjoy?
Support your answer by reference to the text.

OR

(ii)   "In the play, *As You Like It*, Shakespeare upholds the value of romantic love."

Discuss this view of the play, supporting your points by reference to the text.

E   **KING LEAR** – William Shakespeare

(i)   "In the play, *King Lear*, the stories of Lear and Gloucester mirror one another in interesting ways."

Write a response to this view of the play, supporting your answer by reference to the text.

OR

(ii)   "Reading or seeing *King Lear* is a horrifying as well as an uplifting experience."

Write a response to this view, supporting the points you make by reference to the text.

SECTION II

THE COMPARATIVE STUDY (70 marks)

Candidates must answer **one** question from **either A** – Theme or Issue **or B** – The Cultural Context.

In your answer you may not use the text you have answered on in **SECTION I** – The Single Text.

N.B. The questions use the word **text** to refer to all the different kinds of texts available for study on this course, i.e. novel, play, short story, autobiography, biography, travel writing, and film. The questions use the word **author** to refer to novelists, playwrights, writers in all genres, and film directors.

A   THEME OR ISSUE

1.   "In careful reading/viewing of key moments of texts we often find important themes or issues which are developed in the text as a whole."

   (a)   Compare how key moments of two texts you have studied in your comparative course raised an important theme or issue.   (40)

   (b)   In the case of a third text show how a key moment helped in your understanding of the same theme or issue discussed in part *(a)*.   (30)

OR

2.   "The dramatic presentation of a theme or issue can add greatly to the impact of narrative texts."

   Write an essay comparing how the presentation of a theme or issue, common to the texts you have studied for your comparative course, added to the impact of the texts.   (70)

B   THE CULTURAL CONTEXT

1. "The cultural context of a narrative usually determines how the story will unfold."

    (a)   Compare the way in which the cultural context influenced the storyline in **two** of the texts you have studied in your comparative course.

    (40)

    (b)   Show how the cultural context influenced the storyline in a third text you have studied.

    (30)

OR

2. "Understanding the cultural context of a text adds to our enjoyment of a good narrative."

    In the light of the above statement write an essay comparing the cultural contexts of the texts you have studied in your comparative course. Support the comparisons you make by reference to the texts.   (70)

SECTION III

POETRY (70 marks)

Candidates must answer **A** – Unseen Poem **and B** – Prescribed Poetry.

A   UNSEEN POEM (20 marks)

Answer **either** Question **1 or** Question **2**.

The Toy Horse

Somebody, when I was young, stole my toy horse,
The charm of my morning romps, my man's delight.
For two days I grieved, holding my sorrow like flowers
Between the bars of my sullen angry mind.

Next day I went out with evil in my heart,
Evil between my eyes and at the tips of my hands,
Looking for my enemy at the armed stations,
Until I found him, playing in his garden

With my toy horse, urgent in the battle
Against the enemies of his Unreason's land:
He was so happy, I gave him also
My vivid coloured crayons and my big glass marble.

Valentin Iremonger

---

1.   Do you think the poem gives a surprising insight into a childhood experience?
In your answer you might consider:
-        *the pattern of the child's thinking*
-        *the words and images in the poem.*

(20)

OR

2.   Write a response to the above poem, highlighting aspects of it that you liked and/or
disliked.

(20)

B   PRESCRIBED POETRY (50 marks)

Candidates must answer **one** of the following questions (**1 – 4**).

1.   Write an introduction to the poetry of John Donne for new readers.

   Your introduction should cover the following:

   - *The ideas that were most important to him.*
   - *How you responded to his use of language and imagery.*

   Refer to the poems by John Donne that you have studied.

2.   "What Thomas Hardy's poetry means to me."

   Write an essay in response to the above title.

   Your essay should include a discussion of his themes and the way he expresses
   them. Support the points you make by reference to the poetry on your course.

3.   "Reading the poetry of Elizabeth Bishop."

   Write out the text of a talk that you would give to your class in response to the
   above title.

   Your talk should include the following:

   - *Your reactions to her themes or subject matter.*
   - *What you personally find interesting in her style of writing.*

   Refer to the poems by Elizabeth Bishop that you have studied.

4.   "Writing to Michael Longley."

   Write a letter to Michael Longley telling him about your experience of
   studying his poetry. In your letter you should refer to his themes and the way
   he expresses them. Support the points you make by reference to the poetry on
   your course.

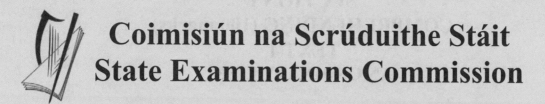

Coimisiún na Scrúduithe Stáit
State Examinations Commission

LEAVING CERTIFICATE EXAMINATION, 2005

English – Higher Level – Paper I

Total Marks: 200

Wednesday, 8th June – Morning, 9.30 – 12.20

- This paper is divided into two sections,
  Section I COMPREHENDING and Section II COMPOSING.
- The paper contains **three** texts on the general theme of ORDINARY LIVES.
- Candidates should familiarise themselves with each of the texts before beginning their answers.

- Both sections of this paper (COMPREHENDING and COMPOSING) must be attempted.
- Each section carries 100 marks.

SECTION I – COMPREHENDING

- Two Questions, A and B, follow each text.
- Candidates must answer a Question A on one text and a Question B on a different text. Candidates must answer only one Question A and only one Question B.
- **N.B.** Candidates may NOT answer a Question A and a Question B on the same text.

SECTION II – COMPOSING

- Candidates must write on **one** of the compositions 1 – 7.

Margaret Forster writes about her grandmother, Margaret Ann Hind, a domestic servant in Carlisle, a town in the north of England, in the 1890s. Her book is called **Hidden Lives – A Family Memoir.**

The life of Margaret Ann, my grandmother, was narrow. The physical hardship, the sheer energy and strength needed to get through each day, was commonplace. She *expected* to be down on her knees scrubbing, up to her elbows in boiling or freezing water, washing and rinsing dishes, rocking on her feet with weariness after hours of running up and down stairs. When she reminisced in later life, it was always without any trace of resentment. Her expectations were low. She was expected to carry on as she was until she dropped. Or married.

Marriage was always an option. Marriage was possibly, but not definitely, or even probably, an escape from servitude. If she married, she knew she'd still have to cook and clean and wash and mend, and without the help of the kind of servant she was to the Stephensons unless she married a rich man. The chances of this happening were nil. Who, in Carlisle, among the servant class, married rich men? Rich, eligible men were few and far between, and girls like Annie Stephenson from good families ever on the lookout for them. But there was rich and rich after all. Plenty of tradesmen around who did quite well for themselves, who could afford to rent or even to buy decent houses and to lead comfortable enough lives. The market was full of them. Plenty of money there, especially among the butchers, with Carlisle being such a big meat-eating place. On Saturday afternoons Margaret Ann would go to the market to buy the meat for Sunday. She went through the glass doors and down the little cobbled hill where the butchers' stalls now were. Some butchers had more than one stall. They had three or four together, positive empires. The meat hung from the ceiling on hooks, whole carcasses of pig and lamb and beef, and on the tiled counters below lay the cut-up portions; the bright red stewing steak, the dark slabs of liver, the great coils of pale, putty-coloured sausage, the crimson mounds of mince, the stiff rows of chops.

Thomas Hind was proprietor of stall number 4. This stall was clean. The carcasses didn't drip blood, the meat on the counter did not lie in puddles of it, the bin for fat wasn't nauseatingly visible. The floor always seemed freshly sawdusted, the aprons of the assistants were spotless. Even though his prices were not the cheapest, there was always a queue at Thomas Hind's. Margaret was a patient queuer. She never attempted to push herself forward but waited her turn calmly. She engaged in none of the banter that other customers seemed to like. She stated her requirement and that was that beyond a please and thank you. These were exactly the qualities which aroused Thomas Hind's interest. He noticed her precisely because of her curious quality of stillness. In 1893, when she first began buying meat from him, he was thirty-five years old and unmarried. His father had been a butcher and so had his grandfather, and as the only son he was always expected to take over the family business. His father had died when Thomas was a child and his mother, Jane, had become a butcher herself in order to keep the business going for Thomas to inherit. His debt to her was strong and he acknowledged it by now supporting not just her but two of his three sisters (the third had married). He was prosperous enough by then to marry. He was notoriously hard to satisfy and was teased about his high standards by his sisters who despaired of him ever approving of any girl. For four years he observed Margaret Ann quite contentedly, and then, when his mother died in 1897, decided the time had come for him to court her very seriously. Nothing impetuous about Tom.

So it was a slow affair, this courtship, three years of best boned and rolled sirloin, shoulder of lamb, leg of pork, three years of pounds of sausage, best back bacon, ham on the bone. A lot of meat, a lot of pleasantries, a lot of cap-doffing on Tom's part and head-inclining on Margaret Ann's. One Saturday, towards the end of the afternoon, when there were no assistants to hear and smirk, no customer other than Margaret Ann to hear and speculate, he asked her if she would care to go with him and his sisters out to Burgh marsh for a breath of sea air. He was very much afraid she would refuse, even be offended, but no, she smiled and said she knew his sisters from church and would be glad to accompany them if she could get time off.

N.B. **Candidates may NOT answer Question A and Question B on the same text.**

Questions A and B carry 50 marks each.

QUESTION A

(i) Write a paragraph in which you comment on the appropriateness of the title of this text, "An Ordinary Life". (15)

(ii) What impressions of the characters of Thomas Hind and Margaret Ann do you get from this passage? Give reasons for your answer. (15)

(iii) Did the description of the market bring it to life for you as a reader? Support your answer by reference to the text. (20)

QUESTION B

"On Saturday afternoons Margaret Ann would go to the market to buy the meat for Sunday."
Write **three diary entries** that Margaret Ann might have written over a series of Saturday evenings. Your writing should relate to her experience as described in the passage.

(50)

TEXT 2
ORDINARY LIVES IN WAR TIME

The following text consists of a written and visual element. The written text is adapted from an introduction by documentary photographer, Jenny Matthews, to her book of photographs entitled **Women and War.**

Mozambique 1986. Soldier with his baby son just before he returns to the front next morning.

El Salvador 1986. An afternoon dance.

Bosnia 1994. Twenty-year-old Spanish soldier serving with UN waving Red Cross convoy over narrow bridge.

Eritrea 1988. Fighter back at base after battle.

INTRODUCTION by Jenny Matthews

From the beginning I was interested in covering foreign stories – starting with Central America in the early eighties, a bit off the map for the British media but an exciting place with revolutionary groups fighting guerrilla wars in the mountains.

One visit led to another and I learned about war. Although I have often worked where pictures in the news were of the frontline confrontation, I was more interested in what was going on behind the scenes, and that usually involved looking at how women were holding everything together. Some of the wars that I've tiptoed around have been major international conflicts – the Balkans, Middle East, Rwanda, Afghanistan – but others have been practically invisible.

I have not been everywhere and this is not a complete record of world conflict; it is my take on recent history, recognising the lives of remarkable women, ordinary people surviving as best they can. As I've travelled I've kept diaries, and the notes from these accompany the photos. All my work has been done in co-operation with a network of people, journalists, friends, fixers, drivers, translators, development workers. Without them it would be hard even to leave home. It has been a great privilege for me to be a photographer, to wander into other people's lives, often uninvited, but usually made embarrassingly welcome. I have lurked around some nasty corners of the world and come across the raw edges of life and death; an infinity of sorrow and fear, but more often than not, tempered with the hope that things will be better for the next generation.

N.B.   Candidates may NOT answer Question A and Question B on the same text.

Questions A and B carry 50 marks each.

QUESTION A

(i)   Which of the four images on page 4 makes the strongest impact on you? Give a reason for your answer.   (15)

(ii)   Do you think that the introduction to the collection of images is an interesting portrayal of Jenny's life as a news photographer? Give reasons for your answer.

(15)

(iii)   "I learned about war … [but] I was more interested in what was going on behind the scenes." From your reading of the introduction **and** the photographs, what impression do you have of how people's lives are touched by war?   (20)

QUESTION B

Write a letter to a photographic magazine in which you propose **one** of the four images for the award **"Best War Photograph of the Year."**   (50)

TEXT 3
PUBLIC LIVES

Some people's lives seem far from ordinary. Modelled on articles from a number of celebrity magazines, the text below was written by a Leaving Certificate student. It offers a glimpse into the lifestyle of imaginary rock star, Eva Maguire.

World exclusive ! Irish Rock Diva speaks to readers from her Italian villa.

Hi, my name is Jerry Philips.
I interview sport stars, superstars, rock stars, divas, celebrities. My targets are the super wealthy, the faces of the moment, the famous; extraordinary lives that excite the curiosity and interest of ordinary people. I cover film premieres, music awards, Oscar ceremonies and star-studded parties; the significant global events of the world of entertainment.

This evening, I am in Florence, ensconced in a huge leather armchair in the waterfront palazzo home of Eva Maguire. In a rare, exclusive and candid interview, the 24 year -old rock superstar reveals where she sees her destiny and for the first time shares with "Celebrity" readers some of the secrets of her forthcoming wedding plans.
Our photo shoot shows her posing with one of her pet miniature greyhounds, wearing her favourite Jacqui Getty jewellery and chic designer labels. As we discuss her plans for the future, personal and professional, candles light up her sun-baked, marble terrace with its glorious views over the Arno River,

far from the terrace house of her childhood in a small Irish town. It has been a roller-coaster 18 months for this Irish-born music queen, originally from the midlands. Discovered on Christmas Eve, busking in Covent Garden, her rise to fame has been meteoric. She has achieved head-spinning, global success, winning international music awards, packing concert venues and seeing her albums topping charts all over the world. Her first CD was the fastest- selling debut album to hit the UK charts and she is fast becoming a rock icon. Her life for the past year has been about L.A., London, New York and Monte Carlo. Some reviewers have criticised her ruthless quest for fame but she is certainly professional, hard-working and determined to succeed in a tough industry. She has been constantly under the media spotlight, (and indeed, some would suggest that today's celebrity culture has gone too far), but says that her stable Irish family background has helped her to cope with the pressures of fame and with the world's press constantly on her doorstep.
"I'm a very reserved person," she says, "but this business is no place to be shrinking and insecure, it takes a certain attitude," she stops and grins. "The point is, I deal with projection all of the time. With a few smart changes, anyone can become a style goddess. Doors have opened for me and I am not afraid to take risks, " she says bluntly.

She is extraordinarily beautiful and astonishingly tough, steely and ambitious. Her golden hair frames features dominated by huge blue eyes. She wears a diamond and sapphire-studded ring on her left hand, reminding us that she is about to marry and share her future with Irish music promoter, Ross Kennedy. 300 Irish friends pack-jammed the luxurious K-Club last weekend in a pre-wedding bash.

International paparazzi are already gathering in the little Italian village where the ceremony will be held. It is expected that a galaxy of Hollywood celebrities, musicians and film producers will attend. It is even rumoured that some surprise politicians will be represented at the wedding. Limousines and helicopters have been arriving at the village for the past 48 hours. About 400 close friends of the couple are flying in from all over the world this weekend.

This spectacular event promises to knock off in style. Expect six hundred doves to flock the Italian sky at the moment when the wedding vows are made and a church filled with tiny rosebuds, orchids and lily-of-the valley. Pink, lilac and white are the colours chosen to predominate this glittering extravaganza. The couple intend to settle on the Italian Riviera. Welcome to their high-octane world of glitz, glamour, sleek yachts and private jets. The honeymoon will begin with a train journey on the Eastern and Oriental express but the ultimate destination is a closely guarded secret. It is expected that the couple will party their way through the coming winter season in Italy.

N.B.   Candidates may NOT answer Question A and Question B on the same text.

Questions A and B carry 50 marks each.

QUESTION A

(i)   How in your view is Jerry Philips's attitude to the rock star, Eva Maguire, revealed in this article? Support your answer by reference to the text.   (15)

(ii)   Does the kind of superstar lifestyle described in this passage appeal to you? Give reasons for your answer, supporting the points you make by reference to the text.   (15)

(iii)   Do you find the style of writing in this magazine article appealing? Support your answer by detailed reference to the text.   (20)

QUESTION B

Imagine that as a reporter for a local newspaper you plan to interview a celebrity of your choice. Write a proposal/memo for the editor of your newspaper in which you explain why you want to interview this celebrity and giving an outline of the areas you hope to explore in the course of the interview.   (50)

SECTION II
COMPOSING (100 marks)

Write a composition on **any one** of the following.

Each composition carries 100 marks.

The composition assignments below are intended to reflect language study in the areas of information, argument, persuasion, narration and the aesthetic use of language.

1.   "… my take on recent history …" (TEXT 2)

   Write a personal essay in which you discuss your views on a recent event or series of events in the world.

2.   "… celebrity culture has gone too far …" (TEXT 3)

   Write a speech in which you attempt to persuade an audience that today's obsession with the lives of the rich and famous has gone too far.

3.   "…ordinary people surviving as best they can."   (TEXT 2)

   You are responding to a radio competition to find an ordinary person whose life story will inspire others. Entries should include an account of the person's life and the reason(s) why it is inspirational. Write your competition entry.

4.   "… the hope that things will be better for the next generation." (TEXT 2)

   Write an article for a newspaper or magazine, outlining your vision of a better future.

5.   "She was expected to carry on as she was ………… he was always expected to take over the family business."   (TEXT 1)

   Write a personal essay on the part which other people's expectations play in our lives.

6.   "She engaged in none of the banter that other customers seemed to like." (TEXT 1)

   You have been asked to give a talk to your class on the importance of not taking life too seriously. Write the talk you would give.

7 (a). **Write a short story suggested by one or more of the images in TEXT 2.**

OR

  (b)   **Write a short story suggested by the pair of images (the two houses) in TEXT 3.**

Coimisiún na Scrúduithe Stáit
State Examinations Commission

LEAVING CERTIFICATE EXAMINATION, 2005

English - Higher Level - Paper 2

Total Marks: 200

Wednesday, 8 June – Afternoon, 1.30 – 4.50

2005

Candidates must attempt the following:-
- **ONE** question from SECTION I – The Single Text
- **ONE** question from SECTION II – The Comparative Study
- **ONE** question on the Unseen Poem from SECTION III – Poetry
- **ONE** question on Prescribed Poetry from SECTION III – Poetry

N.B. Candidates must answer on Shakespearean Drama.
They may do so in SECTION I, The Single Text (*Hamlet, As You Like It*)
or in SECTION II, The Comparative Study (*Hamlet, As You Like It*)

SECTION I

THE SINGLE TEXT (60 marks)

Candidates must answer **one** question from this section (**A – E**).

A **WUTHERING HEIGHTS** – Emily Brontë

    (i)   "Heathcliff deserves the sympathy of the reader of *Wuthering Heights.*"

          Write a response to this statement, supporting your views by reference to the text.

OR

    (ii)   "The novel *Wuthering Heights* portrays a clash between two worlds represented by Wuthering Heights and Thrushcross Grange."

          Discuss this view of the novel, supporting your answer by reference to the text.

B **SILAS MARNER** – George Eliot

    (i)   "The story of *Silas Marner* has the magic of a fairy-tale, which leaves the reader feeling good about people."

          Write a response to this view of the novel, supporting your answer by reference to the text.

OR

    (ii)   "Godfrey Cass is not perfect, but, in the eyes of the reader, he is always a better man than his brother, Dunsey."

          Write your response to this statement, supporting it by reference to the text.

C **AMONGST WOMEN** – John McGahern

    (i)   "Michael Moran undoubtedly loves his sons, but his love contributes little to their happiness."

          Discuss this view of the relationship between Michael Moran and his sons. Support your answer by reference to the text.

OR

    (ii)   "Unlike the men, the women in *Amongst Women* support each other very well."

          Discuss this statement confining your attention to the female characters in the novel. Support your answer by reference to the text.

D   **HAMLET** – William Shakespeare

(i)   In your opinion, what is the appeal of the play, *Hamlet,* for a twenty-first century audience?
Support the points you make by reference to the text.

OR

(ii)   "We admire Hamlet as much for his weaknesses as for his strengths."

Write a response to this view of the character of Hamlet, supporting your points by reference to the text.

E   **AS YOU LIKE IT** – William Shakespeare

(i)   "Rosalind's attitudes and qualities make her a very attractive character."

Do you agree with the above view? Support your answer by reference to the play.

OR

(ii)   "The play, *As You Like It,* presents many opportunities for dramatic performance."

Write your response to the above statement, supporting it by reference to the play.

SECTION II

THE COMPARATIVE STUDY (70 marks)

Candidates must answer **one** question from **either A** – The General Vision and Viewpoint **or B** – Literary Genre.

In your answer you may not use the text you have answered on in **SECTION I** – The Single Text.

N.B. The questions use the word **text** to refer to all the different kinds of texts available for study on this course, i.e. novel, play, short story, autobiography, biography, travel writing, and film. The questions use the word **author** to refer to novelists, playwrights, writers in all genres, and film-directors.

A   THE GENERAL VISION AND VIEWPOINT

1.   "Each text we read presents us with an outlook on life that may be bright or dark, or a combination of brightness and darkness."

In the light of the above statement, compare the general vision and viewpoint in **at least two texts** you have studied in your comparative course.

(70)

OR

2.   *(a)*   With reference to **one** of the texts you have studied in your comparative course, write a note on the general vision and viewpoint in the text and on how it is communicated to the reader.   (30)

(b)   Compare the general vision and viewpoint in **two other texts** on your comparative course. Support the comparisons you make by reference to the texts.   (40)

B   LITERARY GENRE

1.   Write a talk to be given to Leaving Certificate students in which you explain the term *Literary Genre* and show them how to compare the telling of stories in **at least two texts** from the comparative course.   (70)

OR

2.   "Powerful images and incidents are features of all good story-telling."

    (a)   Show how this statement applies to **one** of the texts on your comparative course.   (30)

    (b)   Compare the way in which powerful images and incidents are features of the story-telling in **two other texts** on your comparative course. Support the comparisons you make by reference to the texts.   (40)

SECTION III

POETRY (70 marks)

Candidates must answer **A** – Unseen Poem **and B** – Prescribed Poetry.

A   UNSEEN POEM (20 marks)

Answer **either** Question **1 or** Question **2**.

BACK YARD

Shine on, O moon of summer,
Shine to the leaves of grass, catalpa and oak,
All silver under your rain tonight.

An Italian boy is sending songs to you tonight from an accordion.
A Polish boy is out with his best girl; they marry next month;
      tonight they are throwing you kisses.

An old man next door is dreaming over a sheen
      that sits in a cherry tree in his back yard.

The clocks say I must go – I stay here sitting on the back porch
      drinking white thoughts you rain down.

    Shine on, O moon,
Shake out more and more silver changes.

Carl Sandburg

---

1. *(a)*   Do you like the world that the poet describes in this poem? Give reasons for your answer supporting them by reference to the text.

(10)

    (b)   Choose a line or two that you find particularly appealing and explain why.   (10)

OR

2.   Write a personal response to the poem 'Back Yard'.   (20)

B   PRESCRIBED POETRY (50 marks)

Candidates must answer **one** of the following questions (**1 – 4**).

1.   "The appeal of Eavan Boland's poetry."

Using the above title, write an essay outlining what you consider to be the appeal of Boland's poetry. Support your points by reference to the poetry of Eavan Boland on your course.

2.   What impact did the poetry of Emily Dickinson make on you as a reader? Your answer should deal with the following:

-    *Your overall sense of the personality of the poet*

-    *The poet's use of language/imagery*

Refer to the poems by Emily Dickinson that you have studied.

3.   Write about the feelings that T.S. Eliot's poetry creates in you and the aspects of his poetry (content and/or style) that help to create those feelings. Support your points by reference to the poetry by T.S. Eliot that you have read.

4.   Write an article for a school magazine introducing the poetry of W.B. Yeats to Leaving Certificate students. Tell them what he wrote about and explain what you liked in his writing, suggesting some poems that you think they would enjoy reading. Support your points by reference to the poetry by W.B. Yeats that you have studied.

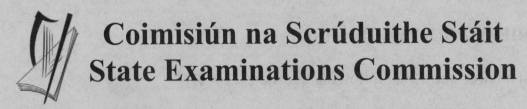

Coimisiún na Scrúduithe Stáit
State Examinations Commission

LEAVING CERTIFICATE EXAMINATION, 2004

English – Higher Level – Paper I

Total Marks: 200

Wednesday, 9th June – Morning, 9.30 – 12.20

- This paper is divided into two sections,
  Section I COMPREHENDING and Section II COMPOSING.
- The paper contains **three** texts on the general theme of WORK AND PLAY.
- Candidates should familiarise themselves with each of the texts before beginning their answers.

- Both sections of this paper (COMPREHENDING and COMPOSING) must be attempted.
- Each section carries 100 marks.

SECTION I – COMPREHENDING

- Two Questions, A and B, follow each text.
- Candidates must answer a Question A on one text and a Question B on a different text. Candidates must answer only one Question A and only one Question B.
- **N.B.** Candidates may NOT answer a Question A and a Question B on the same text.

SECTION II – COMPOSING

- Candidates must write on **one** of the compositions 1 – 7.

SECTION I
COMPREHENDING (100 marks)
TEXT 1
THE IMPORTANCE OF PLAY

The following text is adapted from the writings of Vivian Paley, a teacher who has written over many years about the importance of play in the lives of small children. Paley's books include descriptions of how children play and the stories they tell. The extracts used in this text are taken from her books, **The Boy Who Would Be a Helicopter (1990)** *and* **You Can't Say You Can't Play (1992).**

1. In my early teaching years I paid scant attention to the children's play and did not hear their stories, though once upon a time I too must have invented such wondrous stories. Indeed, my strongest childhood memories are of the daily chase of good and bad guys on the playground. Nothing else mattered, only the play. We acted out fear and friendship and called into being characters who would speak the lines. Luckily, life cannot erase this storytelling instinct; it is always there, waiting to be resurrected.

2. Play is the primary reality of the young school child. Imagine two dozen children in self-selected acting companies, each group performing a different drama, moving through one another's settings, proclaiming separate visions of life and death, inventing new purposes and plots, and no one ever inquires, "What's going on?"
"Y'wanna play tiger? Sabre tooth?"
"Superman! I shotted you."
"Wah, wah, mommy, mommy!"
"Ghostbusters! Green Slimer!"
"Meow, meow, nice kitty."
"Are you the dad, Simon? Here's our cave for good bears."
Not one child asks, "What is everyone doing? Who are these crawling, crouching, climbing people?" There is no confusion, only the desire to fit into someone's story or convince a classmate to enter yours.

3. The deep importance of shared play is clearly evident in the reaction of a child who is told that he or she "can't play", can't be a part of someone else's story. Lately I have become more aware of these voices of exclusion in the classroom. "You can't play" suddenly seems too overbearing and harsh, resounding like a slap from wall to wall. So I propose to my class group that we try out a new rule: You can't say, "you can't play". The children who find the idea appealing are the children most often rejected; the loudest in opposition are those who do the most rejecting. "But then what's the whole point of playing?" Lisa wails.

4. Later, shy Clara speaks for herself. "Cynthia and Lisa builded a house for their puppies and I said can I play and they said no because I don't have a puppy only I have a kitty." This is the longest sentence she has spoken in school to date. "They said I'm not their friend." Clara hugs her tattered kitty and sniffs back her tears.

"We said if she brings in a puppy she can play," Lisa explains. Even the victim does not know how to react. "I'll ask my mommy if she could get me that kind of puppy like they have," Clara offers.

"They has to let her play," Sheila insists, "unless they really don't want to."

"But it was my game!" Lisa cries. "It's up to me!" She is red-faced and tearful. "Okay, I won't play then, ever!"

5. Being told you can't play is a serious matter. It hurts more than anything else that happens in school. Everyone knows the sounds of rejection: You can't play; don't sit by me; stop following us; I don't want you for a partner; you're not going to be on our team.

6. The children I teach are just emerging from life's deep wells of babyhood and family. Then along comes school. It is their first real exposure to the public arena in which everything is to be shared and everyone is meant to be equal. And free acceptance in play, partnerships and teams is what matters most to any child.

N.B.   Candidates may NOT answer Question A and Question B on the same text.

Questions A and B carry 50 marks each.

QUESTION A

(i)   What impression of the teacher, Vivian Paley, do you get from the above passage? Support your view by reference to the text.   (15)

(ii)   From your reading of the passage, what did you learn about the two children, Clara and Lisa?   (15)

(iii)   Would you agree or disagree with the view that the writer has made a convincing case for the 'deep importance of shared play' in the lives of children? Support your point of view by reference to the text.   (20)

QUESTION B

"Then along comes school."

You have been asked to give a short talk to a group of students who are about to start first year in your school. Write out the text of the talk you would give.   (50)

TEXT 2
PAUL'S FIRST DAY AT WORK

The following text is adapted from the novel, **Sons and Lovers,** *by D.H. Lawrence, which tells the story of Paul Morel who, in this extract, begins work at Thomas Jordan & Son— suppliers of elasticated stockings. The novel was first published in 1913.*

On Monday morning, the boy got up at six, to start work. His mother packed his dinner in a small basket, and he set off at a quarter to seven to catch the 7.15 train. Mrs Morel watched him proudly as he trudged over the field. Her elder son, William, was doing well in London and now Paul would be working in Nottingham – her humble contribution to the grandeur of work itself.

At eight o' clock Paul climbed the dismal stairs of Jordan's Factory, and stood helplessly against the first great parcel-rack, waiting for somebody to pick him up. Two clerks had arrived before him and were talking in a corner as they took off their coats and rolled up their shirt sleeves. The younger one spied Paul.

"Hello!" he said. "You the new lad? All right, you come on round here."

Paul was led round to a very dark corner.

"You'll be working with Pappleworth," the young man explained. "He's your boss, but he's not come in yet. So you can fetch the letters, if you like, from Mr Melling down there."

The young man pointed to an old clerk in the office.

"All right," said Paul.

"Here's a peg to hang your cap on—here are your entry ledgers—Pappleworth won't be long."

Paul sat on a high stool and read some of the letters: "Will you please send me at once a pair of lady's silk, spiral thigh stockings, without feet, such as I had from you last year…" or "Major Chamberlain wishes to repeat his previous order for a silk, non-elastic bandage."

He nervously awaited the arrival of his 'boss' and suffered tortures of shyness

when, at half past eight, the factory girls for upstairs trooped past him. Mr Pappleworth arrived at twenty to nine.

"You my new lad?" he said. "Fetched the letters?"

"Yes."

"Copied 'em?"

"No."

Mr Pappleworth sat down beside him, seized the letters, snatched a long entry book out of a rack in front of him, flung it open, seized a pen, and said: "Now look here—you want to copy these letters in here. Think you can do it all right?"

"Yes."

"All right then—let's see you."

Paul rather liked copying the letters, but he wrote slowly, laboriously, and exceedingly badly. He was doing the fourth letter and feeling quite busy and happy, when Mr Pappleworth reappeared.

"Strike my bob, lad, but you're a beautiful writer!" he exclaimed satirically. "How many h'yer done? Only three! I'd 'a eaten 'em.

Come on, my lad, oh, come on... Polly will be crying out for them orders. Here—come out. You'd better watch me do it."

Paul watched the weird little drawings of legs and thighs and ankles which his chief made upon the yellow paper. Mr Pappleworth finished and jumped up.

"Come with me," he said as he dashed through a door, down some stairs and into the basement where a little group of girls, nicely dressed and in white aprons, stood talking together.

"Have you nothing else to do but talk?" said Mr Pappleworth.

"Only wait for you," said one handsome girl, laughing.

"Come on then, Paul," said Mr Pappleworth handing over the orders.

"See you later, Paul," said one of the girls. There was a titter of laughter. Paul went out, blushing deeply, not having spoken a word.

Later, at one o' clock, Paul, feeling very lost, took his dinner basket down into the stack room in the basement, which had the long table on trestles, and ate his meal hurriedly, alone in that cellar of gloom and desolation. At five o'clock all the men went down to the same dungeon and there they had tea, eating bread and butter on the bare dirty boards, talking with the same kind of ugly haste and slovenliness with which they ate their meal. After tea, work went more briskly. Paul made out invoices and prepared his stack of parcels for the post. When the postman finally came everything slacked off and Paul took his dinner basket and, wondering if every work day would be like this, ran to catch the 8.20 train. The day in the factory was just twelve hours long.

N.B. **Candidates may NOT answer Question A and Question B on the same text.**

Questions A and B carry 50 marks each.

QUESTION A

(i) What impression do you get of Paul's workplace from reading the above passage? Support your answer by reference to the text. (15)

(ii) How would you describe the attitudes of the other workers (including Mr Pappleworth) to Paul, the new arrival at Jordan's Factory? Illustrate your answer by reference to the text. (15)

(iii) What advice would you give to the management of Jordan's Factory about how they might improve working conditions for new employees like Paul? (20)

QUESTION B

Employee Assessment

Imagine that Mr Pappleworth is asked, on the basis of Paul's first day at work, to write a report giving his impressions of Paul Morel as an employee. Write the text of his report. (50)

TEXT 3
WORK AND PLAY

The following text consists of a written and a visual element. The visual part of the text is a selection of images of people at work. The written element is an extract from a magazine article on the topic, Work and Play.

Film Director

Actress

Nurse

Lion Tamer

Pilot

Farmer

Professional Sportsman

Company Executive

WORK AND PLAY

There is a natural rhythm to the lives of most people, what we might call the rhythm of work and play, of effort and relaxation, of chore and recreation. For most of us there is a clear dividing line between the work we have to do and our leisure time, the time that is our own exclusively. The division extends also to the kinds of activities that for us constitute work and play. Certainly, there are those among us who seem always to be working, who are so absorbed in work that play can scarcely be said to exist for them. There are those too whose existence seems a perpetual holiday, who are derisively referred to as having 'never worked a day in their lives'.

And there is another group of people who work in areas normally thought of as play, or whose work *is* the play, the recreation of others. Among these we find the professional sportsman or woman, the actor, the filmmaker, the musician, the writer, the comic, the juggler, the high-wire-walker, the lion tamer. These we think of as the lucky ones, the privileged few who turn play itself into work. We imagine them engaged in a kind of work which must always be enjoyable for them and a kind of play that even puts food on the tables of their families. Not for them, it seems, the daily grind from nine to five; not for them the ache of longing for life's all too brief holiday periods. In the eyes of the majority they indeed lead a charmed life, living as they seem to do for the sheer joy of performance!

It is not, however, a matter of carefree play when the professional footballer is dismissed from the field or when the actress fluffs her lines. And I leave it to your imagination to consider the fate that might befall the lion tamer!

N.B.   **Candidates may NOT answer Question A and Question B on the same text.**

Questions A and B carry 50 marks each.

QUESTION A

(i)   What, in your view, is the most important point the writer of the above extract makes about 'the group of people… whose work *is* the play, the recreation of others'?
Support your answer by reference to the text.   (15)

(ii)   What impact does the visual text make upon you? Support your answer by reference to the images.   (15)

(iii)   Do you think that the written and the visual elements of the text go well together? Illustrate your answer by reference to the text as a whole.   (20)

QUESTION B

My Kind of Work

Write a letter to **one** of the people from the collection of visual images in this text, indicating what appeals **and/or** does not appeal to you about the work which that person does.   (50)

SECTION II
COMPOSING (100 marks)

Write a composition on **any one** of the following.

Each composition carries 100 marks.

The composition assignments below are intended to reflect language study in the areas of information, argument, persuasion, narration, and the aesthetic use of language.

1. "… my strongest childhood memories…" (TEXT 1)

   Write a personal essay in which you explore some of your earliest memories of childhood.

2. "Everyone knows the sounds of rejection…" (TEXT 1)

   Write an article for publication in a serious newspaper or journal in which you draw attention to the plight of a person or group of people whom society has rejected.

3. "… the grandeur of work…" (TEXT 2)

   Write a speech (serious or light-hearted) in which you address your classmates or peer-group on the importance of work in our lives.

4. " 'See you later, Paul,' said one of the girls. There was a titter of laughter." (TEXT 2)

   Write a short story suggested by these words.

5. "… the rhythm of work and play..." (TEXT 3)

   Write an article for a magazine for young adult readers in which you give advice to people on the best way to find a healthy balance between work and play in their lives.

6. "… the sheer joy of performance!" (TEXT 3)

   Using the above phrase as your title, write a personal essay.

7. **Write a short story suggested by one or more of the images in TEXT 3.**

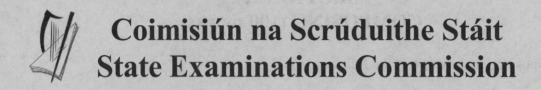

Coimisiún na Scrúduithe Stáit
State Examinations Commission

LEAVING CERTIFICATE EXAMINATION, 2004

English - Higher Level - Paper 2

Total Marks: 200

Wednesday , 9th June – Afternoon, 1.30 – 4.50

Candidates must attempt the following:-

- **ONE** question from SECTION I – The Single Text
- **ONE** question from SECTION II – The Comparative Study
- **ONE** question on the Unseen Poem from SECTION III – Poetry
- **ONE** question on Prescribed Poetry from SECTION III – Poetry

N.B. Candidates must answer on Shakespearean Drama.

They may do so in SECTION I, The Single Text (*Macbeth*)

or in SECTION II, The Comparative Study (*King Lear, Macbeth, Twelfth Night*)

SECTION I

THE SINGLE TEXT (60 marks)

Candidates must answer **one** question from this section (**A – E**).

A   WUTHERING HEIGHTS – Emily Brontë

(i)   "Emily Brontë's novel, *Wuthering Heights,* causes the reader to wonder which is the more powerful force – love or hate."

Write a response to this statement, supporting your views by reference to the text.

OR

(ii)   Write an essay on the aspects of the novel, *Wuthering Heights,* that you found most interesting or enjoyable to read. Support your points by reference to the text.

B   SILAS MARNER – George Eliot

(i)   "The novel *Silas Marner* has much to teach us about the importance of love for human happiness."

Discuss this view of the novel, supporting your answer by reference to the text.

OR

(ii)   "The life lived by the people of Raveloe is an appealing one."

Write a response to this view of the novel, *Silas Marner,* supporting your answer by reference to the text .

C   A DOLL'S HOUSE – Henrik Ibsen

(i)   "Nora retains our sympathy at the end of the play but Torvald does not."

To what extent would you agree with this view? Support your answer by reference to the play.

OR

(ii)   "The relationship between Nora and Torvald is powerfully conveyed in the title of the play, *'A Doll's House'.*"

Write a response to this statement, supporting your views by reference to the text.

D   **AMONGST WOMEN** – John McGahern

(i)   "*Amongst Women* is a powerful portrayal of a family whose world has its joys and its sorrows."

Discuss this view of the novel, supporting your points by reference to the text.

OR

(ii)   "Of all the members of the Moran family, it is Rose, Michael's wife, who most deserves our admiration."

Write a response to this view of Rose, supporting your points by reference to the text.

E   **MACBETH** – William Shakespeare

(i)   "Shakespeare's *Macbeth* invites us to look into the world of a man driven on by ruthless ambition and tortured by regret."

Write a response to this view of the play, *Macbeth*, supporting the points you make by reference to the text.

OR

(ii)   "The play, *Macbeth*, has many scenes of compelling drama."

Choose one scene that you found compelling and say why you found it to be so. Support your answer by reference to the play.

SECTION II

THE COMPARATIVE STUDY (70 marks)

Candidates must answer **one** question from **either A** – Theme or Issue **or B** – Literary Genre.

In your answer you may not use the text you have answered on in **SECTION I** – The Single Text.

N.B. The questions use the word **text** to refer to all the different kinds of texts available for study on this course, i.e. novel, play, short story, autobiography, biography, travel writing, and film. The questions use the word **author** to refer to novelists, playwrights, writers in all genres, and film-directors.

A   THEME OR ISSUE

1.   "Exploring a theme or issue through different texts allows us to make interesting comparisons."

Write an essay comparing the treatment of a single theme that is common to the texts you have studied for your comparative course.

(70)

OR

2.   "Any moment in a text can express a major theme or issue."

    (a)   Choose a moment from each of two texts you have studied for your comparative course and compare the way these moments express the same theme or issue.

(40)

    (b)   Show how a third text you have studied expresses the same theme or issue through a key moment.

(30)

B   LITERARY GENRE

1.   "Literary Genre is the way in which a story is told."

Choose **at least two** of the texts you have studied as part of your comparative course and, in the light of your understanding of the term Literary Genre, write a comparative essay about the ways in which their stories are told. Support the comparisons you make by reference to the texts.   (70)

OR

2.   "Texts tell their stories differently."

(a)   Compare **two** of the texts you have studied in your comparative course in the light of the above statement.   (40)

(b)   Write a short comparative commentary on a third text from your comparative study in the light of your answer to question (a) above.   (30)

SECTION III

POETRY (70 marks)

Candidates must answer **A** – Unseen Poem **and B** – Prescribed Poetry.

A   UNSEEN POEM (20 marks)

Answer **either** Question **1 or** Question **2**.

Margaret Walker is an African American poet. In this poem she celebrates the experiences of the African Americans.

I WANT TO WRITE

I want to write
I want to write the songs of my people.
I want to hear them singing melodies in the dark.
I want to catch the last floating strains from their sob-torn

   throats.

I want to frame their dreams into words; their souls into

   notes.

I want to catch their sunshine laughter in a bowl;
fling dark hands to a darker sky
and fill them full of stars
then crush and mix such lights till they become
a mirrored pool of brilliance in the dawn.

1.   Write a response to the above poem, highlighting the impact it makes on you.   (20)

OR

2.   *(a)*   Write down one phrase from the poem that shows how the poet feels about her people. Say why you have chosen this phrase.   (10)

    (b)   Does this poem make you feel hopeful or not hopeful? Briefly explain why.

    (10)

B   PRESCRIBED POETRY (50 marks)

Candidates must answer **one** of the following questions (**1 – 4**).

1.   "There are many reasons why the poetry of Gerard Manley Hopkins appeals to his readers."

      In response to the above statement, write an essay on the poetry of Hopkins. Your essay should focus clearly on the reasons why the poetry is appealing and should refer to the poetry on your course.

2.   Imagine you were asked to select one or more of Patrick Kavanagh's poems from your course for inclusion in a short anthology entitled, "The Essential Kavanagh".

      Give reasons for your choice, quoting from or referring to the poem or poems you have chosen.

3.   "Speaking of Derek Mahon…"
      Write out the text of a public talk you might give on the poetry of Derek Mahon. Your talk should make reference to the poetry on your course.

4.   "I like (**or** do not like) to read the poetry of Sylvia Plath."

      Respond to this statement, referring to the poetry by Sylvia Plath on your course.

Coimisiún na Scrúduithe Stáit
State Examinations Commission

LEAVING CERTIFICATE EXAMINATION, 2003

English – Higher Level – Paper I

Total Marks: 200

Wednesday, 4th June – Morning, 9.30 – 12.20

- This paper is divided into two sections,
  Section I COMPREHENDING and Section II COMPOSING.
- The paper contains **three** texts on the general theme of JOURNEYS.
- Candidates should familiarise themselves with each of the texts before beginning their answers.

- Both sections of this paper (COMPREHENDING and COMPOSING) must be attempted.
- Each section carries 100 marks.

SECTION I – COMPREHENDING

- Two Questions, A and B, follow each text.
- Candidates must answer a Question A on one text and a Question B on a different text. Candidates must answer only one Question A and only one Question B.
- **N.B.** Candidates may NOT answer a Question A and a Question B on the same text.

SECTION II – COMPOSING

- Candidates must write on **one** of the compositions 1 – 7.

SECTION I
COMPREHENDING (100 marks)
TEXT 1
THE FIRST GREAT JOURNEY

The following is an extract from **The Jason Voyage** *in which the author, Tim Severin, sets out to test whether the legendary journey of Jason's search for the Golden Fleece could have happened in fact. The book was published in 1985.*

It was King Pelias who sent them out. He had heard an oracle which warned him of a dreadful tale – death through the machinations of the man whom he should see coming from the town with one foot bare... The prophecy was soon confirmed. Jason, fording the Anaurus in a winter spate, lost one of his sandals, which stuck in the bed of the flooding river, but saved the other from the mud and shortly appeared before the king. And no sooner did the king see him than he thought of the oracle and decided to send him on a perilous adventure overseas. He hoped that things might so fall out, either at sea or in outlandish parts, that Jason would never see his home again.

1.   So begins the first voyage saga in western literature: the tale of Jason and the Argonauts in search of the Golden Fleece. It tells of a great galley manned by heroes from ancient Greece, which sets out to reach a land far in the east. There, in the branches of an oak tree on the banks of a great river, hangs a sacred fleece of gold, guarded by an immense serpent. If the heroes can bring home the fleece, Prince Jason, the one-sandalled man, will win back his rightful throne from his half-uncle, the usurper King Pelias. On their voyage, so the story recounts, the heroes meet all manner of adventures: they land on an island populated only by women who are eager to make husbands of the Argonauts; a barbaric tribal chieftain challenges them to a boxing match, the loser of which will be battered to death; the dreadful Clashing Rocks bar their path and only by a whisker do they save their vessel from being smashed to shards. A blind prophet, who is being tormented by winged female demons, gives them guidance; and when the heroes finally reach the far land, the king's daughter, Princess Medea, falls so madly in love with Jason that she betrays her family, helps Jason steal the fleece, and flees back with him to Greece.

2.   Small wonder that such an epic tale has echoed down through the centuries. Homer said that it was already a 'tale on all men's lips' when he came to write the *Odyssey*. And now, twenty-two centuries later, my companions and I also set out to commemorate those heroes of old, but in a different manner. Whereas storytellers and poets had accompanied the Argonauts in verse, we hoped to track them in reality. So we rowed out aboard the replica of a galley of Jason's day, a twenty-oared vessel of 3000-year-old design, in order to seek our own Golden Fleece – the facts behind the story of Jason and the Argonauts. Our travel guide was a copy of the *Argonautica*, a book by the Greek poet Apollonius, wrapped in layers of plastic to guard it from the rain and sea spray aboard an open boat. Pessimists calculated that unless favourable winds helped us on our way, we would have to row more than a million oar strokes per man to reach our goal.

3. Our galley, the new *Argo*, was a delight to the eye. Three years of effort had been devoted to her research, design and construction, and now her elegant lines repaid every minute of that care. Fifty-four feet long, from the tip of her curious snout-like ram to the graceful sweep of her tail, she looked more like a sea animal than a ship. On each side the oars rose and fell like the legs of some great beast creeping forward across the quiet surface of the dark blue Grecian sea. Two painted eyes stared malevolently forward over the distinctive nose of her ram, and at the very tip of that ram a hollow handhold breathed like a nostril, as it burbled and snorted with the water washing through the cavity.

4. To me, the tale of Jason and the quest for the Golden Fleece had long held a special fascination. Like most people I first read about Jason in school, but as a historian of exploration studying the great voyage epics of literature, I began to realise just how important the Jason story is. It holds a unique position in western literature as the earliest epic story of a voyage that has survived. The actual ship that carried the heroes, the immortal *Argo*, is the first vessel in recorded history to bear a name. To a seaman this has powerful appeal: for the first time a boat is something more than an inanimate floating object, an anonymous vehicle. *Argo* is a named, identifiable boat that has a character of her own. In the ancient telling of the story *Argo* could speak with a human voice, and at crucial moments state her own opinions. Even the description of her crew as the 'Argonauts' or 'Sailors of *Argo*', comes from the boat herself. In a modern world accustomed to hearing of astronauts, cosmonauts, and even aquanauts, it was worth remembering that the Argonauts were the first epic adventurers of the distant past.

N.B.   Candidates may NOT answer Question A and Question B on the same text.

Questions A and B carry 50 marks each.

QUESTION A

(i)   "Small wonder that such an epic tale has echoed down through the centuries."
How, in Paragraph 1 (beginning "So begins the first voyage saga …"), does the writer establish the truth of this statement?   (15)

(ii)   How, in the course of this extract, does the writer establish links between the voyage of Jason's *Argo* and the voyage of his own boat, the new *Argo*?   (15)

(iii)   Would your reading of the above extract from Tim Severin's book encourage you to read that book in full?
Give reasons for your answer supporting them by reference to the extract.   (20)

QUESTION B

A Journey Through Time
Imagine that you have discovered a time capsule containing a number of items from the distant **or** more recent past. Write a letter to a local or national newspaper announcing your find and describing the items contained in the capsule.   (50)

TEXT 2
A STRANGE COMPANION

This extract is adapted from **The Golden Horde, Travels from the Himalaya to Karpathos,** *published in 1997, in which sixty-five year old Sheila Paine describes her travels through some of the turbulent territories of the former Soviet Union. The extract begins at the point when Sheila returns to Saratov station to try once again to buy a ticket for a train journey.*

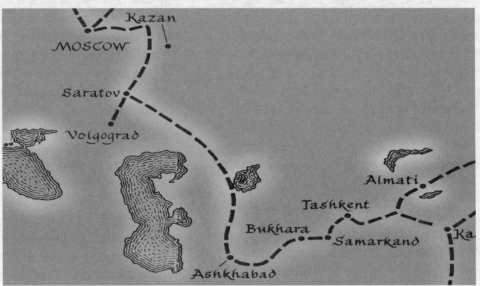

The scene at Saratov station was exactly as I had left it, as if none of the crowds had ever managed to get tickets or to go home or to depart on trains. I joined the battle to buy a ticket once more until, totally exasperated, I was driven to shout out loud, 'God, where do they find these people?' Behind me a voice repeated, 'Yes, God, where are they finding these people?' I turned to see a slim, fine-featured girl with a long blonde ponytail, wearing heavy mountaineering boots, jeans and anorak, and carrying a massive orange rucksack. She held out her hand. 'I'm Alexandra', she said.

I had a travelling companion.

Alexandra had taken a year off studying to travel. She had huge funds of energy but very little money. 'I need no money', she said. 'I am of those travellers who live with the inhabitants.'

At the end of three further hours of queuing and pleading, the woman behind the grille was still saying *niet* – no. During my attempts to buy a ticket I tried to look rather lost and forlorn and held up my money deferentially, bleating 'Ashkhabad please'. Alexandra's approach was spectacularly different. She pummelled her rucksack, kicked the wall with her hefty boots, flung her passport to the ground, screamed 'I kill these people', clenched her fists and punched the grille. However, neither of our techniques worked until Alexandra said, 'You have twenty dollars?' 'Yes', I replied handing her a particularly crisp clean note. Some time later she returned grinning broadly and waving two tickets. 'We just didn't understand the system', I said.

In all travelling it's usually best to go along with whatever the wind blows you and, as Alexandra had by total chance become part of my journey, I decided to stick with her and just see how things went. I had never met anybody quite so extraordinary and, although she might spell trouble later, she had succeeded in getting us on the train from Moscow to Ashkhabad. As we went to board the train I noticed that right at the end of the platform there was a scene of mayhem. A rusty coach with missing windows and our number on it had been tagged on to the train and was already full. Old women were being pushed through the windows head first, their boots and woolly stockings dangling above the platform. Alexandra went to work with her boots on the dense mass of people at the carriage door and we finally found our places in an open compartment with four bunks. Men lay draped on the luggage racks like leopards lounging on tree branches, some sat on the floor and others were piled on our bed. Now Alexandra used her rucksack to push them along and by the time the train pulled out the passengers had, by some hefty manipulation on her part, been reduced to those with places – the two of us, an old lady nursing toothache in a sparkly scarf, two polite young Turkmen – and an assortment of shifty men with no tickets and dozens of boxes of smuggled cigarettes.

We were to be on the train for three days and three nights.

The train trundled through golden open steppeland. At various stations people sold small silvery salted fish, cucumbers, tomatoes and beer. The old lady with the toothache shared her crushed hard-boiled eggs. Alexandra produced a huge bag of boiled millet, a dry loaf and a big silver knife. The men in the luggage racks leant down and helped themselves to everything. I rubbed vodka on the old lady's tooth and gave her aspirin.

The train chugged on. Men on horseback rode over the steppe herding their horses and sheep. The scene had changed from Russian to Mongol. At night it was bitterly cold as the wind howled through the glassless window. 'You should think to bring your sleeping bag', said Alexandra.

By the second morning tempers were frayed. The old lady had produced more hard-boiled eggs, Alexandra her millet and bread. Then, suddenly all hell broke loose.

'I kill him. My knife. Where is my knife? I kill who steals it.'

Boots and arms lashed out, eyes stared down. Then, plop, in all the thrashing the knife fell from the grasp of a fat-lipped luggage-rack man on to the bed below.

The old lady got off the train in the night at one of the bleak Soviet towns along the banks of the Amu Darya river. A miserable place, she had said, and so far from her daughter in Saratov. The polite young Turkmen had helped her off while the fat-lipped thief on the rack above had grabbed her bed. He was now fast asleep.

'Some poor girl will be married off to him', I said.

At the thought of this Alexandra leapt up, threw his baggage off our beds on to the floor and hid his shoes further along the coach.

N.B.   **Candidates may NOT answer Question A and Question B on the same text.**

Questions A and B carry 50 marks each.

QUESTION A

(i)   What impression do you get of the railway station at Saratov from your reading of the above extract? Support your answer by reference to the text.   (15)

(ii)   To what extent would you agree with Sheila's description of Alexandra as 'extraordinary'? Support your view by reference to the text.   (15)

(iii)   Would you like to have shared this train journey with Sheila and Alexandra? Give reasons for your answer.   (20)

QUESTION B

You have been asked to give a short talk on radio about an interesting journey you have made. Write out the text of the talk you would give.   (50)

TEXT 3
DESTINATIONS

other worlds

holidaying in Ireland

European city

winter sports

camping holiday

desert trek

N.B.   **Candidates may NOT answer Question A and Question B on the same text.**

Questions A and B carry 50 marks each.

QUESTION A

(i)   Write **one paragraph** that would serve as an introduction to this collection of images entitled, **Destinations**.   (15)

(ii)   Choose **one** of the images and write an account of the kind of journey suggested by it.
                                                                                                                              (15)

(iii) Briefly describe another destination that would fit in well with the collection printed here and give a reason for your choice.   (20)

QUESTION B

The Holiday from Hell
Write three or four diary entries that record the details of a disastrous holiday (real or imaginary) that you experienced.   (50)

SECTION II
COMPOSING (100 marks)

Write a composition on **any one** of the following.

Each composition carries 100 marks.

The composition assignments below are intended to reflect language study in the areas of information, argument, persuasion, narration and the aesthetic use of language.

1. Imagine you are a member of Tim Severin's crew on board the new *Argo* in TEXT 1.

    Write a letter (or series of letters) to a personal friend or family member in which you describe some of your adventures.

2. "It tells of a great galley manned by heroes from ancient Greece." (TEXT 1)

    Write a persuasive article or essay in which you attempt to convince people of the meaning and importance of heroes in life.

3. "...a tale on all men's lips..." (TEXT 1)

    Write a newspaper article in which you outline your views in a serious or light-hearted manner on the part played by story telling or gossip in everyday life.

4. "We just didn't understand the system." (TEXT 2)

    You have been asked by the school principal to give a talk to your class group on the importance in life of "understanding the system". Write out the talk you would give.

5. "...huge funds of energy but very little money." (TEXT 2)

    Using this as your title, write a personal essay.

6. "In all travelling it's usually best to go along with whatever the wind blows you..." (TEXT 2)

    Write an article for a magazine for young adult readers in which you give advice to people intending to travel abroad for work or on holiday.

7. **Write a short story suggested by one or more of the images in TEXT 3.**

Coimisiún na Scrúduithe Stáit
State Examinations Commission

Leaving Certificate Examination, 2003

English - Higher Level - Paper 2

Total Marks: 200

Wednesday, 4th June – Afternoon, 1.30 – 4.50

Candidates must attempt the following:-

- **ONE** question from SECTION I – The Single Text
- **ONE** question from SECTION II – The Comparative Study
- **THE QUESTIONS** on the Unseen Poem from SECTION III – Poetry
- **ONE** question on Prescribed Poetry from SECTION III – Poetry

N.B. Candidates must answer on Shakespearean Drama.
They may do so in SECTION I, The Single Text (*Macbeth*)
or in SECTION II, The Comparative Study (*Macbeth, Othello, Twelfth Night*)

INDEX OF SINGLE TEXTS

SECTION I

THE SINGLE TEXT (60 marks)

Candidates must answer **one** question from this section (**A – E**).

A WUTHERING HEIGHTS – Emily Brontë

(i) "*Wuthering Heights* is a novel full of passionate extremes."

Write a response to the above statement supporting your views by reference to the text.

OR

(ii) "The novel, *Wuthering Heights*, is dominated from start to finish by the character of Heathcliff."

To what extent would you agree with the above view of the novel? Support your answer by reference to the text.

B THE REMAINS OF THE DAY – Kazuo Ishiguro

(i) "*The Remains of the Day* is a fascinating study of lost potential, of what might have been."

Discuss this view of the novel, supporting the points you make by reference to the text.

OR

(ii) Write an essay on one or more aspects of *The Remains of the Day* that particularly appealed to you as a reader. Support your answer by reference to the text.

C DEATH OF A SALESMAN – Arthur Miller

(i) "*Death of a Salesman* is a tragedy about an ordinary man in an unforgiving world."

What is your opinion of this assessment of the play? Support your answer by reference to the play.

OR

(ii) "BIFF: We never told the truth for ten minutes in this house!"

What do you think of this judgement of the Loman family? Support your answer by reference to the play.

D   AMONGST WOMEN – John McGahern

(i)   "*Amongst Women* is a novel in which everything revolves around the concerns of the central character, Michael Moran."

Write a response to this view of the novel.

OR

(ii)   "Issues of family loyalty are central to *Amongst Women*."

Discuss this view supporting your points by reference to the text.

E   MACBETH – William Shakespeare

(i)   "We feel very little pity for the central characters of Macbeth and Lady Macbeth in Shakespeare's play."

To what extent would you agree with the above view? Support your answer by reference to the play.

OR

(ii)   "In *Macbeth*, Shakespeare presents us with a powerful vision of evil."

Write your response to the above statement. Textual support may include reference to a particular performance of the play you have seen.

SECTION II

THE COMPARATIVE STUDY (70 marks)

Candidates must answer **one** question from **either A** – The Cultural Context **or**
B – The General Vision and Viewpoint.

In your answer you may not use the text you have answered on in **SECTION I** –
The Single Text.

N.B. The questions use the word **text** to refer to all the different kinds of texts available for
study on this course, i.e. novel, play, short story, autobiography, biography, travel, and film.
The questions use the word **author** to refer to novelists, playwrights, writers in all genre, and
film-directors.

A **THE CULTURAL CONTEXT**

1. Write an essay in which you compare the texts you have studied in your
   comparative course in the light of your understanding of the term, the cultural
   context. (70)

OR

2. *(a)* With reference to **one** of the texts you have studied in your comparative
   course, write a note on the way/s in which the cultural context is
   established by the author. (30)

   (b) Compare the ways in which the cultural context is established by the
   authors of **two other texts** on your comparative course. (40)

B   THE GENERAL VISION AND VIEWPOINT

1.   "The general vision and viewpoint of texts can be quite similar or very different."

        In the light of the above statement, compare the general vision and viewpoint in at least two texts on your comparative course.   (70)

OR

2.   *(a)*   What did you enjoy about the exploration of the general vision and viewpoint in **any one** of the texts you read as part of your comparative study? Support your answer by reference to the text.   (30)

        (b)   Write a short comparison between **two other texts** from your course in the light of your answer to part *(a)* above. Support the comparisons you make by reference to the texts.   (40)

SECTION III
POETRY (70 marks)

Candidates must answer **A** – Unseen Poem **and B** – Prescribed Poetry.

A   UNSEEN POEM (20 marks)

Answer **either** Question **1 or** Question **2**.

The poet, Rosita Boland, reflects on the tragedy of a war-torn region in our world.

BUTTERFLIES

In Bosnia, there are landmines
Decorated with butterflies
And left on the grassy pathways
Of rural villages.

The children come, quivering down
Familiar lanes and fields.
Hands outstretched, they reach triumphant
For these bright, elusive insects –
Themselves becoming wingéd in the act;
Gaudy and ephemeral.

1.   Write a short response to the above poem, highlighting the impact it makes on you.
(20)

OR

2.   Comment on the following statements supporting your answers by reference to the poem, *Butterflies*.

   (a)   The poem makes very effective use of irony.   (10)

   (b)   The poem uses beautiful language to capture an ugly reality.   (10)

B   PRESCRIBED POETRY (50 marks)

Candidates must answer **one** of the following questions (**1 – 4**).

1.   "Why read the poetry of John Donne?"

   Write out the text of a talk that you would give, or an article that you would submit to a journal, in response to the above title. Support the points you make by reference to the poetry of John Donne on your course.

2.   "We enjoy poetry for its ideas and for its language."

   Using the above statement as your title, write an essay on the poetry of Robert Frost. Support your points by reference to the poetry by Robert Frost on your course.

3.   If you were asked to give a public reading of a small selection of Sylvia Plath's poems, which ones would you choose to read? Give reasons for your choices supporting them by reference to the poems on your course.

4.   *Dear Seamus Heaney ...*

   Write a letter to Seamus Heaney telling him how you responded to some of his poems on your course. Support the points you make by detailed reference to the poems you choose to write about.

AN ROINN OIDEACHAIS AGUS EOLAÍOCHTA
LEAVING CERTIFICATE EXAMINATION, 2002

English – Higher Level – Paper I

Total Marks: 200

Wednesday, 5th June – Morning, 9.30 – 12.20

- This paper is divided into two sections,
  Section I COMPREHENDING and Section II COMPOSING.
- The paper contains **three** texts on the general theme of FAMILY.
- Candidates should familiarise themselves with each of the texts before beginning their answers.

- Both sections of this paper (COMPREHENDING and COMPOSING) must be attempted.
- Each section carries 100 marks.

SECTION I – COMPREHENDING

- Two Questions, A and B, follow each text.
- Candidates must answer a Question A on one text and a Question B on a different text. Candidates must answer only one Question A and only one Question B.
- **N.B.** Candidates may NOT answer a Question A and a Question B on the same text.

SECTION II – COMPOSING

- Candidates must write on **one** of the compositions 1 – 7.

The following text consists of a written and a visual element. The written part of this text is adapted from a preface by the American poet, Carl Sandburg, to a collection of photographs entitled **The Family of Man**. The visual images are taken from the exhibition which was first shown in the Museum of Modern Art, New York, in 1955.

2002

PREFACE by Carl Sandburg

The first cry of a newborn baby in Chicago or Zamboango, in Amsterdam or Rangoon, has the same pitch and key, each saying, "I am! I have come through! I belong! I am a member of the Family."

When you look at these images you see that the wonder of human mind, heart, wit and instinct, is here. You might catch yourself saying, "I'm not a stranger here." People, flung wide and far, born into toil, struggle, blood and dreams, among lovers, eaters, drinkers, workers, loafers, fighters, players, gamblers. Here are ironworkers, bridgemen, musicians, sandhogs, miners, builders of huts and skyscrapers, jungle hunters, landlords and landless, the loved and the unloved, the lonely and the abandoned, the brutal and the compassionate – one big family hugging close to the ball of Earth for its life and being.

Here or there you may witness a startling harmony. In a seething of saints and sinners, winners and losers, in a womb of superstition, faith, genius, crime, sacrifice, here is the People, ever lighted by the reality or the illusion of hope. Hope is a sustaining human gift.

Everywhere is love and love-making, wedding and babies from generation to generatio keeping the Family of Man alive and continuing Everywhere the sun, moon and stars, th climates and weathers, have meanings fo people. Though meanings vary, we are alike i all countries and tribes in trying to read wha sky, land and sea say to us. Alike and eve alike we are all on continents in the need of love food, clothing, work, speech, worship, sleep games, dancing, fun. From tropics to arctic humanity lives with these needs so alike, s inexorably alike.

If the human face is "the masterpiece of God" is here then in fateful registrations. Often th faces speak what words can never say. Faces c blossom smiles or mouths of hunger ar followed by homely faces of majesty carved an worn by love, prayer and hope, along with other light and carefree as thistledown in a lat summer wind. They are faces beyond forgetting written over with faith and dreams of mankin surpassing itself. An alphabet is here and multiplication table of living breathing huma faces. An epic woven of fun, mystery an holiness – here is the Family of Man!

N.B. Candidates may NOT answer Question A and Question B on the same text.

Questions A and B carry 50 marks each.

QUESTION A

(i) What impact do the visual images in this text make upon you? Give reasons for your answer supporting them by reference to the images. (20)

(ii) What, in your opinion, is the most important point that Carl Sandburg makes in his preface to the images in the exhibition? (20)

(iii) Do you think that the written and visual elements of the text go well together? Illustrate your answer by brief reference to the text as a whole. (10)

QUESTION B

Choose **one** of the visual images in this text and, in a **letter** to Carl Sandburg, write your response to its inclusion in the exhibition of photographs entitled *The Family of Man*. [The images have been numbered so that you can indicate your choice clearly.] (50)

TEXT 2
FAMILY HOME FOR SALE

Novelist, Penelope Lively, remembers her family home through the wealth of little things it contained.
This article was published in **The Sunday Times** *of August 26, 2001.*

A few years ago, the house in which my grandmother had set up home in 1923 had to be sold. It had seen more than seventy years of occupancy by my family, and hardly a hair of its head had been changed during that time. Everything was still as it had always been – the gong-stand by the front door, the photograph albums in the hall chest, the tarnished contents of the silver cupboard, the horsehair mattress on which I slept in the dressing-room during my school holidays.

This country house, tucked away in West Somerset, had seen out the century, and it reflected seven decades of social change. Its furnishings were a secret message, if you knew how to read the code. The place was eloquent; the old sewing machine in the attic, the bell panel in the pantry, the oil-lamps stashed away on the larder shelves, the faded rosettes in the stables – everything spoke of the way we lived then.

Any house tells a story; its furnishings are a shining reference to some aspect of past habitation. They seem to me to be more than just the backdrop to one family's life, and to bear witness to the events of the past. And in this sense our old home was peculiarly well stocked with archival matter. In a large house with cupboards and disused rooms, things are not discarded, they are simply 'put away'. Seventy years of putting away had created strata from which we retrieved my grandmother's 100-year-old wedding dress, bound volumes of Punch from the 1880s onwards, Thermos flasks of the 1950s, a forest of walking sticks, an army of glass jars for fruit bottling, Primus stoves, preserving pans. Granted reincarnation, I would like to be an archaeologist. There is something extraordinarily emotive and exciting about the deductions that can be made about an entire way of life from a few surviving shards, bones, scraps of metal, shadows on the ground.

Through our family homes most of us have an accumulated freight of objects that speak to us of the life history of our own family, all the bits and pieces that we have acquired ourselves along with the things that have filtered down through the generations – an ancestral desk, a grandmother's necklace, a parent's books or pictures. A number of years ago I visited the Soviet Union, as it then was, with a group of British writers; we were entertained one evening in the flat of one of our hosts – two cramped rooms in which all the furnishings were contemporary and utilitarian. I noticed a pretty 19th century coffee cup. Our hostess told me that it had belonged to her mother: "It is all that she had left from her home, after the war." One coffee cup; I thought of the wealth of physical objects that conjure up other times and other people in a country spared such punishment.

N.B.   **Candidates may NOT answer Question A and Question B on the same text.**

Questions A and B carry 50 marks each.

QUESTION A

(i)   How, in your opinion, does Penelope Lively feel about her family home?
Support your view by detailed reference to the text.   (20)

(ii)   What features of good descriptive writing are to be found in the above passage?
Illustrate the points you make from the text.   (20)

(iii)   Why, in your view, does the writer include the reference to her visit to the Soviet Union?
(10)

QUESTION B

Family Home and Contents for Sale
Drawing on the detail in the above text, and its accompanying illustration, draft the text of an advertisement that offers the home and its contents for sale.

(50)

TEXT 3
FAMILIES IN A TIME OF CRISIS

This text is an extract from the novel, **The Grapes of Wrath,** *by the American writer, John Steinbeck. The novel tells the story of poor farming families who are forced to travel hundreds of miles across America in search of a living. In this extract we learn how the desire of families to support one another leads to the setting up of a society in itself. The novel was first published in 1939.*

The cars of the migrant people crawled out of the side roads on to the great cross-country highway, and they took the migrant way to the West. In the daylight they scuttled like bugs to the westward; and as the dark caught them, they clustered like bugs near to shelter and to water. And because they were lonely and perplexed, because they had all come from a place of sadness and worry and defeat, and because they were all going to a new mysterious place, they huddled together; they talked together; they shared their lives, their food, and the things they hoped for in the new country. Thus it might be that one family camped near a spring, and another camped for the spring and for company, and a third because two families had pioneered the place and found it good. And when the sun went down, perhaps twenty families and twenty cars were there.

In the evening a strange thing happened: the twenty families became one family, the children were the children of all. The loss of home became one loss, and the golden time in the West was one dream. And it might be that a sick child threw despair into the hearts of twenty families, of a hundred people; that a birth there in a tent kept a hundred people quiet and awestruck through the night and filled a hundred people with the birth-joy in the morning. A family which the night before had been lost and fearful might search its goods to find a present for a new baby. In the evening, sitting about the fires, the twenty were one. They grew to the units of the camps, units of the evenings, and the nights. A guitar unwrapped from a blanket and tuned – and the songs, which were all of people, were sung in the nights. Every night relationships that make a world, established; and every morning the world torn down like a circus. At first the families were timid in the building and tumbling worlds, but gradually the technique of building worlds became their technique. Then leaders emerged, then laws were made, then codes came into being. And as the worlds moved westward they were more complete and better furnished, for their builders were more experienced in building them.

The families learned what rights must be observed – the right of privacy in the tent; the right to keep the past hidden in the heart; the right to talk and to listen; the right to refuse help or to accept, to offer or to decline it; the right of son to court daughter and daughter to be courted; the right of the hungry to be fed; the rights of the pregnant and the sick to transcend all other rights. And as the worlds moved westward, the rights became rules, became laws, although no one told the families. And with the laws, the punishments – and there were only two – a quick and murderous fight, or ostracism; and ostracism was the worst. For if one broke the laws his name and face went with him, and he had no place in any world, no matter where created.

There grew up a government in the worlds, with leaders, with elders. A man who was wise found that his wisdom was needed in every camp, and a kind of insurance developed in these nights. A man with food fed a hungry man, and thus insured himself against hunger. And when a baby died a pile of silver coins grew at the door flap of the tent, for a baby must be well buried, since it has had nothing else of life.

N.B. **Candidates may NOT answer Question A and Question B on the same text.**

Questions A and B carry 50 marks each.

QUESTION A

(i)   How does the language of the opening paragraph suggest the powerlessness of the migrant people? Support your answer by reference to the text.

(20)

(ii)   In the remainder of the passage, how does Steinbeck show the bonds between people becoming stronger and more powerful? Support your points by reference to the text.   (20)

(iii)   "There grew up a government in the worlds…" Look again at the final paragraph. What, in your view, is the most important thing it says about people? Explain your answer, illustrating briefly from the text.   (10)

QUESTION B

"Rights Must Be Observed"
You have been asked to give a short talk on radio or television about a fundamental human right that you would like to see supported more strongly. Write out the text of the talk you would give.

(50)

SECTION II
COMPOSING (100 marks)

Write a composition on **any one** of the following.

Each composition carries 100 marks.

The composition assignments below are intended to reflect language study in the areas of information, argument, persuasion, narration and the aesthetic use of language.

1. "…one big family hugging close to the ball of Earth for its life and being…" (TEXT 1)

   Write a personal essay in response to the above phrase.

2. "Hope is a sustaining human gift." (TEXT 1)

   You have been asked to deliver a speech on this theme to a group of young people. Write out the speech you would give.

3. "…the life history of our own family…" (TEXT 2)

   Write an article for a popular magazine or journal in which you explore the aspects of your own family that are special to you. You may, if you wish, write your composition in diary format.
   [N.B. You should not use your own family name.]

4. "…after the war." (TEXT 2)

   Write a short story suggested by the above title.

5. "…relationships that make a world…and … the world torn down like a circus…" (TEXT 3)

   Write an article (serious or humorous) about the beginning and ending of a relationship in your life.

6. "…then laws were made…" (TEXT 3)

   Write a serious article in which you argue for or against the importance of laws in our society.

7. **Write a short story prompted by one or more of the images in TEXT 1.**

An Roinn Oideachais agus Eolaíochta
Leaving Certificate Examination, 2002

English - Higher Level - Paper 2

Total Marks: 200

Wednesday, 5th June – Afternoon, 1.30 – 4.50

Candidates must attempt the following:-

- **ONE** question from SECTION I – The Single Text
- **ONE** question from SECTION II – The Comparative Study
- **THE QUESTIONS** on the Unseen Poem from SECTION III – Poetry
- **ONE** question on Prescribed Poetry from SECTION III – Poetry

N.B. Candidates must answer on Shakespearean Drama.
They may do so in SECTION I, The Single Text (*King Lear, Hamlet*)
Or in SECTION II, The Comparative Study (*Hamlet, Henry V, King Lear, Othello*)

SECTION I

THE SINGLE TEXT (60 marks)

Candidates must answer **one** question from this section (**A – F**).

A **JANE EYRE** – Charlotte Brontë

(i) "While many of the situations that Jane finds herself in are sad and pitiful, she responds to them with strength and independence."

Discuss this statement, supporting your answer by reference to the novel.

OR

(ii) "In the novel, *Jane Eyre*, we meet characters who show us the best and the worst in human nature."

Write a response to this statement, supporting your answer by reference to the novel.

B **GREAT EXPECTATIONS** – Charles Dickens

(i) "The course of the relationship between Pip and Estella makes for wonderful reading."

What is your view of this statement? Refer to the novel in your answer.

OR

(ii) "In *Great Expectations*, Dickens brilliantly describes a world full of cruelty and inequality."

Discuss this assessment of *Great Expectations*. Support your answer by reference to the novel.

C **FAR FROM THE MADDING CROWD** – Thomas Hardy

(i) "Of all the characters (both male and female) we meet in the novel, Gabriel Oak is the real hero."

Write a response to this statement supporting it by reference to the novel, *Far From the Madding Crowd*.

OR

(ii) "In *Far from the Madding Crowd*, Hardy shows he is a superb storyteller who invents fascinating characters and colourful incidents."

Discuss this statement, supporting the points you make by reference to the novel.

D   KING LEAR – William Shakespeare

    (i)   "Powerful images heighten our experience of the play, *King Lear*."

           Write your response to this statement. Textual support may include reference to a particular performance you have seen of the play.

OR

    (ii)   "Cordelia plays a very important role in the play, *King Lear*."

           Discuss this view of Cordelia, supporting your answer by reference to the play.

E   HAMLET – William Shakespeare

    (i)   "The appeal of Shakespeare's *Hamlet* lies primarily in the complex nature of the play's central character, Hamlet."

           To what extent would you agree with the above statement? Support your view by reference to the play.

OR

    (ii)   What is your view of the importance of **either** Gertrude **or** Ophelia in Shakespeare's play, *Hamlet*?

           Support the points you make by reference to the play.

F   ANTIGONE – Sophocles

    (i)   "Creon's unwilling journey from pride and power towards humiliation and weakness leaves him utterly devastated."

           Discuss this view of Creon's journey, supporting your points by reference to the play, *Antigone*.

OR

    (ii)   "The play, *Antigone,* is a tragic struggle between conflicting rights."

           Write a response to this statement, supporting your answer by reference to the play, *Antigone*.

SECTION II

THE COMPARATIVE STUDY (70 marks)

Candidates must answer **one** question from **either A** – Theme or Issue **or B** – The Cultural Context.

In your answer you may not use the text you have answered on in **SECTION I** – The Single Text.

N.B. The questions use the word **text** to refer to all the different kinds of texts available for study on this course, i.e. novel, play, short story, autobiography, biography, travel, and film. The questions use the word **author** to refer to novelists, playwrights, writers in all genre, and film-directors.

A   THEME OR ISSUE

1.   "A theme or issue explored in a group of narrative texts can offer us valuable insights into life."

Compare the texts you have studied in your comparative course in the light of the above statement. Your discussion must focus on **one** theme or issue. Support the comparisons you make by reference to the texts.   (70)

OR

2.   *(a)*   Compare the treatment of a theme or issue in **two** of the texts you have studied as part of your comparative course. Support the comparisons you make by reference to the texts.   (40)

(b)   Discuss the treatment of **the same theme or issue** in a third text in the light of your answer to part *(a)* above.   (30)

B   THE CULTURAL CONTEXT

1.   "A narrative text creates its own unique world in which the reader can share."

Write a response to the above statement in which you compare the texts you have studied as part of your comparative course. Support the comparisons you make by reference to the texts.   (70)

OR

2.   *(a)*   What is your understanding of the term Cultural Context in relation to any **one** of the texts in your comparative course? Support your view by reference to **at least one** key moment from your chosen text.   (30)

(b)   Compare **two other texts** from your comparative course in the light of your understanding of the term Cultural Context as you have discussed it in part *(a)* above. Support the comparisons you make by reference to **at least one** key moment from each of these two texts.   (40)

SECTION III

POETRY (70 marks)

Candidates must answer **A** – Unseen Poem **and B** – Prescribed Poetry.

A **UNSEEN POEM** (20 marks)

Answer questions **1 and 2**.

The poet, Thomas McCarthy, reflects upon the introduction of the euro.

Read the poem at least twice and then answer the questions that follow it.

THE EURO

I've seen the first photograph of the new Euro
in a shop-window in Patrick Street.

Rather than anything that belongs to the future,
it reminds me of the orange ten-shilling note

of my childhood: an orange note
that held the promise of so much happiness.

With a ten-shilling note you could buy
almost anything in Mansfield's shop;

you could take the boat and train to Wembley;
you could secure a bicycle for Christmas
all the way back from the month of September.

I wonder if a boy like myself will think
of a ten-Euro note as something promising –
Though paper money, now, can hardly mean the same

as it did to me, a child of coins.
Somewhere, perhaps in a provincial European city,
in Bologna, maybe, or Antwerp or Nantes,

there is a small boy of ten – a child of coins –
for whom the Euro will come
like a sudden ache of optimism, a sunbeam

to illuminate the cleared path ahead.

I have high hopes for that boy. I honour him.

1. What impact does the first sighting of the new euro make upon the poet?
   Support your answer by reference to the poem. (10)

2. How well, in your view, does the poem capture the sense of excitement and hope that
   the introduction of the euro could hold for "a small boy of ten"? Illustrate your answer
   by reference to the language of the poem. (10)

B PRESCRIBED POETRY (50 marks)

Candidates must answer **one** of the following questions (**1 – 4**).

1. "The poetry of Elizabeth Bishop appeals to the modern reader for many reasons."

    Write an essay in which you outline the reasons why poems by Elizabeth Bishop have this appeal.

2. Write a personal response to the poetry of Eavan Boland.

    Support the points you make by reference to the poetry of Boland that you have studied.

3. Imagine you have invited Michael Longley to give a reading of his poems to your class or group. What poems would you ask him to read and why do you think they would appeal to your fellow students?

4. "Choosing Shakespeare's Sonnets."

    Imagine your task is to make a small collection of sonnets by William Shakespeare from those that are on your course. Write an introduction to the poems that you would choose to include.

AN ROINN OIDEACHAIS AGUS EOLAÍOCHTA
LEAVING CERTIFICATE EXAMINATION, 2001

English – Higher Level – Paper 1

Total Marks: 200

Wednesday, 6th June — Morning, 9.30 – 12.20

- This paper is divided into two sections,
  Section I COMPREHENDING and Section II COMPOSING.
- The paper contains **four** texts on the general theme of IRISHNESS.
- Candidates should familiarise themselves with each of the texts before beginning their answers.

- Both sections of this paper (COMPREHENDING and COMPOSING) must be attempted.
- Each section carries 100 marks.

SECTION I — COMPREHENDING

- Two Questions, A and B, follow each text.
- Candidates must answer a Question A on one text and a Question B on a different text. Candidates must answer only one Question A and only one Question B.
- **N.B.** Candidates may NOT answer a Question A and a Question B on the same text.

SECTION II — COMPOSING

- Candidates must write on **one** of the compositions 1 – 7.

SECTION I
COMPREHENDING (100 marks)

TEXT 1
BEING IRISH

The following extracts are adapted from the book, *Being Irish,* in which a number of contributors give their responses to the question 'What does it mean to be Irish today?' The book was published in 2000, and its editor is Paddy Logue.

Jennifer Johnston, *is a writer and was born in Dublin in 1930.*

I have never found another country in which I would rather live and die. I feel great pride when we do things right and a great anger when we get things horribly wrong. All my bondings have happened in this country, with my family and the past, my city, and the whole landscape of the island, to the language we use and the way we have moulded it and made it different and vital, the stories we tell and the songs we sing and all the people with whom I have learned and worked and played. I feel comfortable here; the shoes of Irishness fit me well. What more can I say?

Polly Devlin, *is a writer, broadcaster and conservationist. She lives in London.*

When I went to London at age nineteen my Irishness became something new in my life — something much less local but not quite real. My being Irish was used as an explanatory sort of fond shorthand among my English peers. The way "she's Irish" or "that's very Irish" was said seemed different from how "she's French" was said. It seemed to me that there was a lot less baggage to being French in England. My nationality seemed more of a personal matter, as though it would account for any unpredictability in my nature. I was both flattered and resentful and, perhaps, being young and isolated, played up to it.

Seán McCague, *is President of the Gaelic Athletic Association.*

The modern Ireland is a thriving economic entity that has still managed to treasure most of its traditions. Our rich cultural heritage has been protected while at the same time we welcome the world onto our shores. There is a unity of mind in being Irish. Our games, our heritage, our music, dance and our built and green heritage are all part of what we are.

Brian Kennedy, *is a singer from Belfast.*

Songs are a safe place to visit how you really feel, regardless of the intensity. In trying to explain being Irish, I would say it's like taking a picture of the word "sadness" and then taking another picture of the word "joy". When the film comes back from the chemist, it has been double-exposed and the two words have become superimposed like some strange hybrid. Someone told me they could hear this in my voice, especially when I sang an old Irish song.

Patricia Harty, *a native of Tipperary, is Editor-in-Chief of* Irish America *magazine.*
My heart lights up when I see another Irish person. I love Irish music, and there are more Irish *seisiúns* in New York than anywhere else. I believe I can tell an Irishman from the way he walks, the way he holds his head. With Irish people so much is left unsaid, or is said with a nod or a wink or an unspoken gesture. Like all people who have faced danger together, the Irish have a highly developed intuitive sense of each other.

Martin Mansergh *is special adviser to the Taoiseach on Northern Ireland, Economic and Social Matters.*
To be Irish today is something to be proud of. It is to be part of a stunningly beautiful country that is a success story on many fronts, the peace process, an economy driven by technological innovation, as well as much cultural and sporting achievement. The resources exist at last to tackle outstanding social problems. Our young people look outwards.

N.B. Candidates may NOT answer Question A and Question B on the same text.

Questions A and B carry 50 marks each.

Question A

(i)   What aspects of Irishness emerge most strongly for you from the above extracts?   (20)

(ii)   In your opinion, which one of the writers expresses his or her sense of Irishness best? Give reasons for your answer supporting it by reference to your chosen extract.   (15)

(iii) Choose **one** of the people in the above text and, based on the views he or she has expressed, write a short account of the kind of person you imagine him or her to be.   (15)

Question B

Imagine your job is to welcome a group of foreign students to Ireland. Write out the text of a short talk (150 – 200 words) in which you advise them how best to get along with the Irish people they will meet.   (50)

2001

TEXT 2
A NEW IRELAND

The following text is adapted from the inauguration speech of President Mary Robinson, the first woman to hold the office of President of Ireland. The speech was delivered on December 3rd, 1990.

Citizens of Ireland, mná na hÉireann agus fir na hÉireann, you have chosen me to represent you and I am humbled by and grateful for your trust.

The Ireland I will be representing is a new Ireland, open, tolerant, inclusive. Many of you who voted for me did so without sharing all my views. This, I believe, is a significant signal of change, a sign, however modest, that we have already passed the threshold to a new, pluralist Ireland. The recent revival of an old concept of the Fifth Province expresses this emerging Ireland of tolerance and empathy. The Fifth Province is not anywhere here or there, north or south, east or west. It is a place within each of us – that place that is open to the other, that swinging door which allows us to venture out and others to venture in. If I am a symbol of anything, I would like to be a symbol of this reconciling and healing Fifth Province.

My primary role as President will be to represent this state. But the state is not the only model of community with which Irish people can and do identify. Beyond our state there is a vast community of Irish emigrants extending not only across our neighbouring island but also throughout the continents of North America, Australia, and of course Europe itself. There are over seventy million people living on this globe who claim Irish descent. I will be proud to represent them.

There is another level of community which I will represent. Not just the national, not just the global, but the local community. Within our state there are a growing number of local and regional communities determined to express their own creativity, identity, heritage and initiative in new and exciting ways. In my travels around Ireland I have found local community groups thriving on a new sense of self-confidence and self-empowerment. Whether it was groups concerned with adult education, employment initiative, women's support, local history and heritage, environmental concern or community culture, one of the most enriching discoveries was to witness the extent of this local empowerment at work. As President I will seek to the best of my abilities to promote this growing sense of local participatory democracy, this emerging movement of self-development and self-expression which is surfacing more and more at grassroots level. This is the face of modern Ireland.

The best way we can contribute to a new and integrated Europe is by having a confident sense of our Irishness. Here again we must play to our strengths – take full advantage of our vibrant cultural resources in music, art, drama, literature, and film; value the role of our educators, promote and preserve our unique environmental and geographical resources of relatively pollution-free lakes, rivers, landscapes and seas; encourage, and publicly support local initiative projects in aquaculture, forestry, fishing, alternative energy and small-scale technology.

I want this Presidency to promote the telling of stories – stories of celebration through the arts and stories of conscience and of social justice. As a woman, I want women who have felt themselves outside history to be written back into history. May I have the fortune to preside over an Ireland at a time of exciting transformation, when we can enter a new Europe where old wounds can be healed, a time when, in the words of Seamus Heaney, "hope and history rhyme".

N.B. Candidates may NOT answer Question A and Question B on the same text.

Questions A and B carry 50 marks each.

Question A

(i)   Basing your answer on the text of the above speech, how do you think Mary Robinson views her role as President of Ireland? Outline your views in 150 to 200 words, supporting your points by reference to the text.   (30)

(ii) To what extent would you find yourself in agreement or disagreement with her view of the role of President? Support your point of view by reference to the text.   (20)

Question B

In the above text, Mary Robinson refers to the importance of "the local community". Write a short article (150 – 200 words) about a project or activity in your local community, which you admire or condemn.

(50)

TEXT 3
AN IRISH SENSE OF HUMOUR

The following text is a narrative (in abridged form) taken from the poet Ciaran Carson's book *The Star Factory* which tells the story of Ulster and its people. The author tells us he received this story from his father. The book was first published in 1997.

Johnny McQueen and Agnes Reed were married during the war. Times were hard for them and they wished for nothing better than a home of their own. One morning Johnny spotted a little cottage that was up for rent in Mullaghbawn, with half an acre attached. The pair wasted no time, and the next day they were installed in their own little house.

One night, as he was sitting by the fire contentedly smoking his pipe, Johnny announced that he would go to Newry to buy a spade or a shovel to 'do something with that half-acre out there'.

Next day Johnny went into Newry town and brought back what he needed. He was no sooner home than he went out the back and started to dig. A couple of hours went by and when Agnes looked out she couldn't see Johnny at all, he was down in this great hole, digging for all he was worth. So out she goes, and says:

'What in God's name are you at, at all?'

Johnny emerges from the hole and stands looking at it proudly.

'By God,' says he, 'isn't that a beautiful hole?'

'What use is it? What can you do with it?' says Agnes.

'I know what I can do with it,' says Johnny, 'I can put it in the paper and sell it, that's what I'll do'.

The next day Paddy Murphy was eating his breakfast and reading the *Frontier Sentinel* in his house in Newry town.

'Listen to this, Kathleen,' he says to his wife, 'here's the most peculiar ad I've seen in a long while: SUPERLATIVE HOLE FOR SALE; ALL ENQUIRIES TO "FOUR WINDS", MULLAGHBAWN, CO. ARMAGH. I think I'll take a run over there right now and see what it's all about.'

It wasn't long till Paddy stood outside McQueen's. He knocked on the door and Johnny came out.

'Are you the man that has the hole?' says Paddy.

'I am,' says McQueen, 'are you interested?'

He took Paddy out and showed him the hole.

'By God,' says Paddy, 'I never saw such a hole in my life. She must be thirty foot deep.'

'She is,' says Johnny, 'and maybe more. Are you for buying?'

'I am, surely,' says Paddy, 'how much are you looking?'

'Well, she's worth twenty pound, for she took me the guts of a whole day digging her, but seeing I'm a Newry man myself, I'll let her go for ten.'

'Fair enough,' says Murphy, 'it's a deal. But how will I get her home to Newry?'

'Well,' says Johnny, 'there's always the Ulster Transport Authority.'

So Paddy landed at the UTA depot in Newry and he said to the clerk: 'I'm just after buying this hole beyond in Mullaghbawn, and I'd like to hire a lorry and six men to bring her back to Newry.'

'That's all in order,' says the clerk, 'I'll have a lorry and a gang of men out there in no time, and you should have the hole some time tomorrow afternoon.'

Next day Paddy spent the whole afternoon pacing the floor waiting for the hole to arrive. Night came and there was no word of the hole. So, next morning he went to the UTA office and demanded to speak to the manager.

'It's like this,' says Paddy, 'I bought a hole beyond in Mullaghbawn, and I was looking forward to having her installed in the front garden, and I hired a lorry and six men in this very office for the job, and damn the hole I've seen yet. What kind of service do you call that?'

'You're right,' says the manager, 'this won't do at all.' And he called over to the clerk for an explanation.

'Oh,' says the clerk, 'are you the man that bought the hole? Well, I sent out a lorry and a gang of men, and after struggling with the hole for seven hours, they eventually succeeded in placing her on the back of the vehicle; but there's a wild steep incline between Mullaghbawn and Newry, and the hole fell off the back of the lorry. The men were trying their level best to get the hole back on, when the lorry fell into the hole. The men then tried to haul the lorry out of the hole, but fell in themselves, and we haven't seen sight nor hair of them since!'

N.B. Candidates may NOT answer Question A and Question B on the same text.

Questions A and B carry 50 marks each.

Question A

(i) Where in this story, did it first strike you that it was going to be a funny tale? Account for your answer.

(10)

(ii) In the remainder of the story, what are the signals that let you know it is intended to be a humorous story?

(20)

(iii) Write a paragraph (100 – 150 words) in which you comment on the appropriateness of the title, "An Irish Sense of Humour".

(20)

Question B

Imagine your local radio station is producing a programme entitled *COMIC MOMENTS* in which a person from the community introduces his/her favourite comic moment from the world of radio, television, or live performance. Write the text (150 – 200 words) of the presentation you would like to make.

(50)

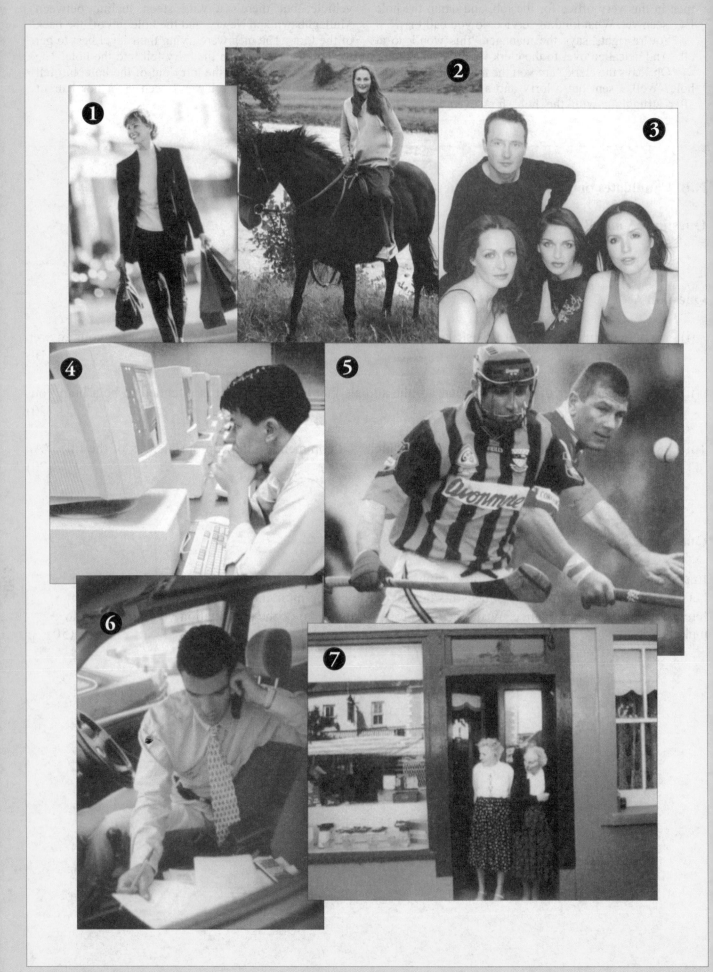

N.B. Candidates may NOT answer Question A and Question B on the same text.

Questions A and B carry 50 marks each.

Question A

(i) Taking all of the above images into account, in your opinion what overall picture of Ireland is projected in this visual text? Outline your views in 150 – 200 words, supporting your points by reference to the images. (20)

(ii) (*a*) Imagine this series of images is to be used in a brochure whose objective it is to promote Ireland abroad. Which one of the images would you choose for its front cover? Justify your choice. (15)

(*b*) You are the editor of the brochure mentioned in part (a). Which one of the images would you judge to be **least representative** of the Ireland you wish to promote? Justify your choice. (15)

Question B

A Day in the Life

Choose **one** of the people pictured in TEXT 4 and write **four** short diary entries that your chosen person might write on **one important day** in his/her life. You should indicate clearly the person you have chosen and you should write the diary entries as though you were that person. (50)

SECTION II
COMPOSING (100 marks)

Write a composition on **any one** of the following.

Each composition carries 100 marks.

The composition assignments below are intended to reflect language study in the areas of information, argument, persuasion, narration, and the aesthetic use of language.

1. "Citizens of Ireland…you have chosen me to represent you…" (TEXT 2)

    You have been elected President of Ireland. Write the first speech you would make to the Irish people.

2. "The shoes of Irishness fit me well." (Jennifer Johnston, TEXT 1)

    Write a personal essay in which you explore your sense of what it means to be Irish.

3. "Our games are…part of what we are." (Seán McCague, TEXT 1)

    Write an article intended for inclusion in the sports pages of a newspaper in which you attempt to persuade your readers of the value of sport in our lives.

4. "Songs are a safe place to visit how you really feel." (Brian Kennedy, TEXT 1)

    Write an article for your school or local magazine in which you explore your feelings about the place of music and/or songs in your life.

5. "Our young people look outwards." (Martin Mansergh, TEXT 1)

    Write a letter to Martin Mansergh in which you outline your response to his view of young Irish people.

6. "An Irish Sense of Humour." (TEXT 3)

    Write a narrative similar in style to the story told in TEXT 3.

7. **Write a short story prompted by one or more of the images in TEXT 4.**

AN ROINN OIDEACHAIS AGUS EOLAÍOCHTA
LEAVING CERTIFICATE EXAMINATION, 2001

English – Higher Level – Paper 2

Total Marks: 200

Wednesday, 6th June — Afternoon, 1.30 – 4.50

Candidates must attempt the following: —
- **ONE** question from SECTION I — The Single Text
- **ONE** question from SECTION II — The Comparative Study
- **THE QUESTIONS** on The Unseen Poem from SECTION III — Poetry
- **ONE** question on Prescribed Poetry from SECTION III — Poetry

N.B. Candidates must answer on Shakespearean Drama.

They may do so in SECTION I, The Single Text (*King Lear, Hamlet*)

Or in SECTION II, The Comparative Study (*Hamlet, Henry V, King Lear, Othello*)

2001

SECTION I

THE SINGLE TEXT (60 marks)

Candidates must answer **one** question from this section (**A — F**).

A   JANE EYRE — Charlotte Brontë

(i)   "Despite great changes in her life's circumstances, Jane Eyre remains true to herself."

Do you agree with this view of Jane? Support your answer by reference to the novel.

OR

(ii)   "Injustice is a major feature of the world of Charlotte Brontë's *Jane Eyre*."

Discuss this view of the novel, supporting your answer by reference to the text.

B   GREAT EXPECTATIONS — Charles Dickens

(i)   "Magwitch's act of generosity towards Pip has both negative and positive effects on the development of Pip's character throughout the novel."

Discuss this statement, supporting your answer by reference to the novel.

OR

(ii)   "*Great Expectations* is a masterpiece, full of memorable incidents and bizarre characters."

Do you agree with this assessment of the novel? Support your answer by reference to the novel.

C   FAR FROM THE MADDING CROWD — Thomas Hardy

(i)   What is your view of the decisions Bathsheba makes in matters of romance and affairs of the heart? Support your answer by reference to the novel.

OR

(ii)   "The characters, Oak, Troy and Boldwood, represent different aspects of male behaviour and values."

Discuss this statement supporting your points by reference to the novel.

D   KING LEAR — William Shakespeare

(i)   What, in your view, are the most important changes that take place in the character of Lear during the play, *King Lear*? Support your points by reference to the play.

OR

(ii)   "Scenes of great suffering and of great tenderness help to make *King Lear* a very memorable play."

Discuss this statement, supporting your answer by reference to the play, *King Lear*.

E   HAMLET — William Shakespeare

(i)   "The struggle between Hamlet and Claudius is a fascinating one."

Discuss this statement, supporting your answer by reference to the play, *Hamlet*.

OR

(ii)   Choose the scene from Shakespeare's *Hamlet* that in your view was the most dramatic. Discuss your choice, supporting your answer by reference to the play. [Textual support may include reference to a particular performance of the play that you have seen.]

F   ANTIGONE — Sophocles

(i)   "*Antigone* is memorable for its ideas and for its dramatic action."

Discuss this statement, supporting your answer by reference to the play.

OR

(ii)   How would you judge the attitudes and behaviour of the character of Antigone throughout Sophocles's play? Support your views by reference to the text.

SECTION II

THE COMPARATIVE STUDY (70 marks)

Candidates must answer **one** question from **either A** — Theme or Issue **or B** — Literary Genre.

In your answer you may not use the text you have answered on in **SECTION I** — The Single Text.

N.B. The questions use the word **text** to refer to all the different kinds of texts available for study on this course, i.e. novel, play, short story, autobiography, biography, travel and film. The questions use the word **author** to refer to novelists, playwrights, writers in all genre, and film-directors.

A   THEME OR ISSUE

1.   "Narratives can broaden our understanding of a theme or issue."

   Compare the texts you have studied in your comparative course in the light of the above statement. Support your comparisons by reference to the texts.   (70)

OR

2.   "A key moment in a narrative text can illustrate a theme or issue very powerfully."

   (*a*)   Choose **one** of the texts you studied as part of your comparative course and show how an important moment from it illustrates a theme or issue.   (30)

   (*b*)   Write a short comparative commentary on **one key moment** from each of the other texts you have studied in the light of your discussion in part (a) above.   (40)

B   LITERARY GENRE

1.   Write an essay on **one or more** of the aspects of literary genre (the way texts tell their stories) which you found most interesting in the texts you studied in your comparative course. Your essay should make clear comparisons between the texts you choose to write about.   (70)

OR

2.   "No two texts are exactly the same in the manner in which they tell their stories."

(*a*)   Compare **two** of the texts you have studied in your comparative course in the light of the above statement. Support the comparisons you make by reference to the texts.   (40)

(*b*)   Write a short comparative commentary on a third text from your comparative study in the light of your discussion in part (a) above.   (30)

SECTION III

POETRY (70 marks)

Candidates must answer **A** – Unseen Poem **and** B – Prescribed Poetry.

A   UNSEEN POEM (20 marks)

Answer questions **1** and **2**.

In this poem by Edna St Vincent Millay the princess recalls a moment that fills her with sadness.

Read the poem at least twice and then answer the questions that follow it.

THE PRINCESS RECALLS HER ONE ADVENTURE

Hard is my pillow
Of down from the duck's breast,
Harsh the linen cover;
I cannot rest.

Fall down, my tears,
Upon the fine hem,
Upon the lonely letters
Of my long name;
Drown the sigh of them.

We stood by the lake
And we neither kissed nor spoke;
We heard how the small waves
Lurched and broke
And chuckled in the rock.

We spoke and turned away.
We never kissed at all.
Fall down, my tears.
I wish that you might fall
On the road by the lake,
Where my cob* went lame,   * a horse
And I stood with the groom
Till the carriage came.

1. (*a*)   What, in your opinion, has made the princess sad?   (4)

    (*b*)   Choose two phrases from the poem that show best how she is feeling. Write each one
            down and say, in each case, why you have chosen it.   (6)

2. What kind of life do you imagine the princess lives? Explain your view by referring to
    words or phrases from the poem.   (10)

B   PRESCRIBED POETRY (50 marks)

Candidates must answer **one** of the following questions (**1 — 4**).

1. "Introducing Elizabeth Bishop."

    Write out the text of a short presentation you would make to your friends or class group under the above title. Support your point of view by reference to or quotation from the poetry of Elizabeth Bishop that you have studied.

2. Often we love a poet because of the feelings his/her poems create in us. Write about the feelings John Keats's poetry creates in you and the aspects of the poems (their content and/or style) that help to create those feelings. Support your points by reference to the poetry by Keats that you have studied.

3. Write an essay in which you outline your reasons for liking and/or not liking the poetry of Philip Larkin. Support your points by reference to the poetry of Larkin that you have studied.

4. What impact did the poetry of Michael Longley make on you as a reader? In shaping your answer you might consider some of the following:

    —   *Your overall sense of the personality or outlook of the poet*
    —   *The poet's use of language and imagery*
    —   *Your favourite poem or poems.*

2001

English - Higher Level - Paper 1

SAMPLE PAPER

Total Marks: 200

Time: 2¹/₂ hours

- This paper is divided into two sections,
  Section I COMPREHENDING and Section II COMPOSING.
- The paper contains **four** texts on the general theme of OUR WORLD.
- Candidates should familiarise themselves with each of the texts before beginning their answers.

- Both sections of this paper (COMPREHENDING and COMPOSING) must be attempted.
- Each section carries 100 marks.

SECTION I - COMPREHENDING
- Two Questions, A and B, follow each text.
- Candidates must answer a Question A on one text and a Question B on a different text.
- **N.B.** Candidates may NOT answer a Question A and a Question B on the same text.

SECTION II - COMPOSING
- Candidates must write on **one** of the compositions 1-7.

SECTION I
COMPREHENDING (100 marks)

TEXT 1
OUR WORLD - THEIR WORLD

The following text is adapted from a table compiled by journalist Paul Cullen.
The table appeared in *The Irish Times* of December 31 1999.

OUR WORLD	THEIR WORLD
• The world's population today: 6,034,867,134	• 1.3 billion people live on less than $1 a day
• Just over four babies are born every second - 131 million a year	• About 840 million people are malnourished
• Republic of Ireland's population: 3,632,944 (July 1999 est.)	• 100 million of the world's people are homeless
• 1 per cent of the richest 200 people's wealth would pay for access to primary education for all	• One in five of the world's children of primary school age is out of school
• Americans spend $8 billion a year on cosmetics	• In New York City, 52% of children are born into poverty
• Europeans spend $11 billion annually on ice-cream	• 11 people are infected with AIDS /HIV every minute; 95 per cent of cases occur in developing countries
• Annual spending on pet foods in Europe and the US: $17 billion	• AIDS causes 2.3 million deaths a year
• Europeans spend $50 billion on cigarettes	• Nearly 13 million children have been orphaned by AIDS
• Military spending in the world is $780 billion per year	• 8,000 to 10,000 children are maimed or killed by landmines every year
• Four diseases nearly eradicated: polio, guinea worm, neonatal tetanus, leprosy	• Four diseases identified since 1995: nipah virus, avian flu, new variant CJD, Kaposi sarcoma virus
• There are currently 300 million mobile phone users; by 2003 there will be one billion	• 3,000 of the world's 6,000 languages are endangered
• The illegal drugs trade accounts for 8% of world trade, or $400 billion a year	• Since 1970 40 per cent of the world's forests have disappeared

N.B. Candidates may NOT answer Question A and Question B on the same text.

Questions A and B carry 50 marks each.

QUESTION A

(i) What general conclusions do you draw from the above table of information? Outline your view in 150 to 200 words, illustrating the points you make by reference to the text.   (30)

(ii) What, in your view, is the author's purpose in laying out the information in the format used in the text? Support your point of view by detailed reference to at least two entries in the text.   (20)

QUESTION B

Based on the information given in TEXT 1, complete the following tasks:-

(i) Draft a **brief set of guidelines** intended to make the world a more just place in which to live.

(10)

(ii) With reference to any **one of your guidelines** write a letter to a politician, at local or national level, explaining your point of view and encouraging him/her to adopt your policy as a matter of urgency.   (40)

TEXT 2
SOPHIE'S WORLD

This text is taken from the opening chapters of *Sophie's World*, a novel by Jostein Gaarder about the history of philosophy. The novel, first published in 1991, tells the story of Sophie Amundsen, a young girl who receives letters from a mysterious stranger. The letters try to interest her in philosophy and they offer her a course of instruction in the important questions that philosophers ask.

Dear Sophie,

1.   Lots of people have hobbies. Some people collect old coins or foreign stamps, some do needlework, others spend most of their spare time on a particular sport. If I happen to be interested in horses or precious stones, I cannot expect everyone else to share my enthusiasm. Is there, though, nothing that interests us all? Is there nothing that concerns everyone - no matter who they are or where they live in the world? Yes, dear Sophie, there are questions that certainly should interest everyone. They are precisely what this course is about.

2.   There is something that everyone needs, and that is to figure out who we are and why we are here. Being interested in why we are here is not a casual interest like collecting stamps. People who ask such questions are taking part in a debate that has gone on as long as man has lived on this planet. How the universe, the earth, and life came into being is a bigger and more important question than who won the most gold medals in the last Olympics.

Questioning

3.   The best way of approaching philosophy is to ask a few philosophical questions: How was this world created? Is there any will or meaning behind what happens? Is there a life after death? How can we answer these questions? And most important, how ought we to live? People have been asking these questions throughout the ages. We know of no culture which has not concerned itself with what man is and where the world came from. Basically there are not many philosophical questions to ask. We have already asked some of the most important ones. But history presents us with many different answers to each question. So it is easier to ask philosophical questions than it is to answer them.

It begins with wonder

4.   A Greek philosopher who lived more than two thousand years ago believed that philosophy had its origin in man's sense of wonder. Man thought it was so astonishing to be alive that philosophical questions arose of their own accord. It is like watching a magic trick. We cannot understand how it is done. So we ask: how can the magician change a couple of white silk scarves into a live rabbit? A lot of people experience the world with the same incredulity as when a magician suddenly pulls a rabbit out of a hat which has just been shown to them empty. In the case of the rabbit, we know the magician has tricked us. What we would like to know is just how he did it. But when it comes to the world it's somewhat different. We know that the world is not all sleight of hand and deception because here we are in it, we are part of it. Actually, we *are* the white rabbit being pulled out of the hat. The only difference between us and the white rabbit is that the rabbit does not realise it is taking part in a magic trick. Unlike us. We feel we are part of something mysterious and we would like to know how it all works.

5.   As far as the white rabbit is concerned, it might be better to compare it with the whole universe. We who live here are microscopic insects existing deep down in the rabbit's fur. But philosophers are always trying to climb up the fine hairs of the fur in order to stare right into the magician's eyes.

N.B. Candidates may NOT answer Question A and Question B on the same text.

Questions A and B carry 50 marks each.

QUESTION A

(i) Based on your reading of the above text what do you understand the term philosophy to mean?
(15)

(ii) What is the letter-writer's attitude to philosophy and to the questions it asks? (15)

(iii) How well, in your view, do the references to the rabbit in paragraphs 4 and 5 help to define the nature of philosophers? (20)

QUESTION B

Thought for Today - How we ought to live

You have been asked by your local radio station to give a one or two minute talk to early-morning listeners on your philosophy of life. Write the script (150 - 200 words) of the talk you would deliver. (50)

TEXT 3
THE LIBRARY

The setting of the gothic novel *Titus Groan* by Mervyn Peake is Gormenghast, the vast crumbling castle of the hero, Titus Groan. In this scene we meet Lord Sepulchrave, father of Titus, in the towering library. The novel was first published in 1946.

1. The Library

The library stood between a building with a grey dome and one with a façade that had once been plastered. Most of the plaster had fallen away, but scraps had remained scattered over the surface, sticking to the stones. Patches of faded colour showed that a fresco had once covered the entire face of the building. Neither doors nor windows broke the stone surface. On one of the larger pieces of plaster that had braved a hundred storms and still clung to the stone, it was possible to make out the lower part of a face, but nothing else was recognisable among the fragments.

The library, though a lower building than these two to which it was joined at either end, was of a far greater length than either. The track that ran alongside the eastern wing, now in the forest and now within a few feet of the kaleidoscopic walls shadowed by the branches of the evergreens, ended as it curved suddenly inwards towards the carved door. Here it ceased among the nettles at the top of the three deep steps that led down to the less imposing of the two entrances to the library, but the one through which Lord Sepulchrave always entered his realm. It was not possible for him to visit his library as often as he wished, for the calls made upon him by the endless ceremonials which were his exacting duty to perform robbed him for many hours each day of his only pleasure - books.

2. The Melancholy of Sepulchrave

This evening found Lord Sepulchrave free at seven and sitting in the corner of his library, sunk in a deep reverie. The room was lit by a chandelier whose light, unable to reach the extremities of the room, lit only the spines of those volumes on the central shelves of the long walls. A stone gallery ran round the library at about fifteen feet above the floor, and the books that lined the walls of the main hall fifteen feet below were continued upon the high shelves of the gallery. In the middle of the room, immediately under the light, stood a long table. It was carved from a single piece of the blackest marble, which reflected upon its surface three of the rarest volumes in his Lordship's collection.

Upon his knees, drawn up together, was balanced a book of his grandfather's essays, but it had remained unopened. His arms lay limply at his side, and his head rested against the velvet of the

chair back. He was dressed in the grey habit which it was his custom to wear in the library. From full sleeves his sensitive hands emerged with the shadowy transparency of alabaster. For an hour he had remained thus; the deepest melancholy manifested itself in every line of his body.

The library appeared spread outwards from him as from a core. His dejection infected the air about him and diffused its stillness upon every side. All things in the long room absorbed his melancholia. The shadowing galleries brooded with slow anguish; the books receding into the deep corners, tier upon tier, seemed each a separate tragic note in a monumental fugue of volumes.

3. The Marriage

It was only on those occasions now, when the ritual of Gormenghast dictated, that he saw the Countess.

They had never found in each other's company a sympathy of mind or body, and their marriage, necessary as it was from the lineal standpoint, had never been happy. In spite of his intellect, which he knew to be far and away above hers, he felt and was suspicious of the heavy, forceful vitality of his wife, not so much a physical vitality as a blind passion for aspects of life in which he could find no cause for interest. Their love had been passionless, and save for the knowledge that a male heir to the house of Groan was imperative, they would have gladly forgone their embarrassing yet fertile union. During her pregnancy he had only seen her at long intervals. No doubt the unsatisfactory marriage had added to his native depression, but compared with the dull forest of his inherent melancholy it was but a tree from a foreign region that had been transplanted and absorbed.

N.B. Candidates may NOT answer Question A and Question B on the same text.

Questions A and B carry 50 marks each.

QUESTION A

(i)   What kind of world do you think has been created by the author in the above extract? (15)

(ii) Outline briefly your feelings towards the character of Sepulchrave as you encounter him in the above passage. Support your viewpoint by brief reference to the text. (15)

(iii) What features of good descriptive writing did you find in the above passage? Support your points by illustrative detail from the text. (20)

QUESTION B

Imagine that Lord Sepulchrave has decided to sell the castle of Gormenghast. Using the above text and the accompanying illustrations, write, in 150 - 200 words, the text of the advertisement that might appear in the property pages of a newspaper. (50)

TEXT 4
EXPLORING OUR WORLD

N.B. Candidates may NOT answer Question A and Question B on the same text.

Questions A and B carry 50 marks each.

QUESTION A

(i)   What kinds of exploration of our world are suggested to you by the images in TEXT 4?   (10)

(ii) What image of exploration appeals to you most? Outline your response in around 50 words.   (10)

(iii) Does this set of images represent for you a harmonious or a conflicting view of our world?   (10)
      Support your view by reference to the images.

(iv) Imagine this visual is to appear in a current affairs journal or magazine.
      Write a short text (100 - 150 words) to accompany it.   (20)

QUESTION B

The following short letter (169 words) condemning mankind's advances in science and technology has appeared in a newspaper.

Dear Sir,

I, for one, am feeling heartily sick at the constant stream of boasting about scientific advancements being made in the modern world. If we are not busy cloning sheep and other innocent creatures we are mucking about on factory-style farms injecting harmless vegetables with hormones, trying to turn them into so-called super vegetables. What or whose interests are being served by all this 'progress', I wonder?

Surely it is time to face up to the awkward fact that for centuries now the world *has* been discovered! We don't need to make any further discoveries in the name of science or any other name. What we need to do now is share the natural fruits of the world fairly among *all* the citizens of the world. We desperately need to return to a time when we could feel the solid earth beneath our feet, breathe in the clean air around us, and look up in wonder at the vastness of the sky above!

Yours in ever diminishing hope.

Write to the newspaper a letter of your own (150 - 200 words) in which you challenge or support the views outlined by the above writer.   (50)

SECTION II
COMPOSING (100 marks)

Write a composition on **any one** of the following.

Each composition carries 100 marks.

The composition assignments below are intended to reflect language study in the areas of information, argument, persuasion, narration, and the aesthetic use of language.

1. '100 million of the world's people are homeless' (TEXT 1)

   Write an argument, intended for publication in a serious newspaper or journal, in which you outline your views on the manner in which life can be improved for the world's poor.

2. Ours is a consumer-driven world.

   'Europeans spend $11 billion annually on ice-cream'
   'Annual spending on pet foods in Europe and the US: $17 billion'
   'Europeans spend $50 billion on cigarettes' (TEXT 1)

   Write a personal essay for your school magazine in which you consider some implications (serious and/or humorous) of the above extracts from Text 1.

3. 'There are currently 300 million mobile phone users; by 2003 there will be one billion' (TEXT 1)

   Write an article for a popular magazine in which you outline your views on the impact of the mobile phone in the home, school, and/or workplace.

4. The letter-writer in TEXT 2 argues that philosophy has 'its origin in man's sense of wonder'.

   Write a composition in which you attempt to persuade your readers that mankind has or has not lost its sense of wonder.

5. **A group of tourists arrives to spend a weekend in Gormenghast, the castle in TEXT 3. Write the story of the events that unfold as you would imagine them.**

6. 'His exacting duty...robbed him for many hours each day of his only pleasure - books.' (TEXT 3)

   Write an article intended for publication in your school magazine or local newspaper encouraging people to spend more of their leisure time reading.

7. **Write a narrative that establishes a link between two or more of the images in TEXT 4.**

AN ROINN OIDEACHAIS AGUS EOLAÍOCHTA
LEAVING CERTIFICATE EXAMINATION

English – Higher Level – Paper 2

SAMPLE PAPER

Total Marks: 200

Time: 3 hours

Candidates must attempt the following: —
- **ONE** question from SECTION I — The Single Text
- **ONE** question from SECTION II — The Comparative Study
- **THE QUESTIONS** on the Unseen Poem from SECTION III — Poetry
- **ONE** question on Prescribed Poetry from SECTION III — Poetry

N.B. Candidates must answer on Shakespearean Drama.
They may do so in SECTION I, The Single Text (*King Lear, Hamlet*)
Or in SECTION II, The Comparative Study (*Hamlet, Henry V, King Lear, Othello*)

SECTION I

THE SINGLE TEXT (60 marks)

Candidates must answer **one** question from this section (**A — F**).

A   JANE EYRE — Charlotte Brontë

(i)   "Jane's intelligence and sense of self-respect enable her to determine her future in a way that beauty and wealth could not."

Do you agree with this view of Jane? Support your answer by reference to the novel.

OR

(ii)   What impressed you most about Charlotte Brontë's novel *Jane Eyre?* Support your view by reference to the text.

B   GREAT EXPECTATIONS — Charles Dickens

(i)   "Dickens makes excellent use of caricatures to add drama and humour to *Great Expectations.*"

Discuss this statement, supporting your answer by reference to the novel.

OR

(ii)   "Despite his early selfishness and snobbishness, Pip does earn our admiration."

Do you agree with this assessment of Pip? Support your answer by reference to the novel.

C   FAR FROM THE MADDING CROWD — Thomas Hardy

(i)   "Bathsheba's self-reliance and her vulnerability make her attractive to the male characters, Oak and Troy."

Discuss this statement, supporting your answer by reference to the novel.

OR

(ii)   "The search for love preoccupies the main characters in *Far From the Madding Crowd.*"

Discuss this statement in relation to any **two** characters from the novel. Support your answer by reference to the novel.

D   KING LEAR — William Shakespeare

   (i)   "The play *King Lear* offers us characters who represent the very worst and the very best in human nature."

          Do you agree with this statement? Support your answer by reference to the play.

                                          OR

   (ii)   "The play *King Lear* offers us one central experience — pessimism."

          Write a response to this statement. Support your answer by reference to the play.

E   HAMLET — William Shakespeare

   (i)   "For some people Claudius is a black-hearted villain who is justly punished for the murder of his brother, while for others he is a potentially good king who pays dearly for his past."

          Which of these two views of Claudius would you favour more? Support your discussion by reference to the play. (N.B. In your answer you may discuss **one or both** of the above views of the character.)

                                          OR

   (ii)   "There are many comic moments in Shakespeare's *Hamlet.*"

          Discuss this statement supporting your points by reference to the play.

F   ANTIGONE — Sophocles

   (i)   "Sophocles, the author of *Antigone,* presents to his audience a very bleak view of the world."

          To what extent would you agree with the above view of the play? Support your points by reference to the play.

                                          OR

   (ii)   Discuss the importance of the Chorus in *Antigone*. Support your points by reference to the play.

SECTION II

THE COMPARATIVE STUDY (70 marks)

Candidates must answer **one** question from **either** A — Literary Genre **or** B — The Cultural Context.

In your answer you may not use the text you have answered on in **SECTION I** — The Single Text.

N.B. The questions use the word **text** to refer to all the different kinds of texts available for study on this course, i.e. novel, play, short story, autobiography, biography, travel and film. The questions use the word **author** to refer to novelists, playwrights, writers in all genre, and film-directors.

A LITERARY GENRE

1. "All readers enjoy a story that is well told."

    Taking the above statement as your theme write an essay in which you compare the ways in which the texts in your comparative study told their stories. (70)

OR

2. Choose **one** of the following aspects of literary genre as your topic and answer questions (*a*) **and** (*b*): —

    — *The use of powerful imagery*

    — *The creation of memorable characters*

    (*a*) Compare the presence of your chosen topic in **two** of the texts you have studied as part of your comparative course. Illustrate your comparisons by reference to **at least one key moment** from each text. (40)

    (*b*) Consider some similarities **and/or** differences in the way in which a **third** text deals with the same topic. Support your points by brief textual reference. (30)

B   THE CULTURAL CONTEXT

1.   (*a*)   Choose any **one** of the texts you studied as part of your comparative course and describe how aspects of the cultural context shaped the overall atmosphere of the narrative. Illustrate your points by reference to **one or more key moments** from the text.   (30)

      (*b*)   Write a short comparative commentary on **one or more** of the other texts on your course in the light of your discussion of the text you have chosen for part (*a*) above.   (40)

OR

2.   The author of a narrative text creates a world (a cultural context) in which the story unfolds. Using **one** key moment from each of three texts you studied in your comparative course, compare the impact of the cultural context on **one** of the following areas: —

      — *determining events in the lives of the characters*

      — *making the stories more realistic or credible*

      — *heightening the impact of the stories on the reader.*   (70)

SECTION III

POETRY (70 marks)

Candidates must answer A – Unseen Poem **and** B – Prescribed Poetry

A.   UNSEEN POEM (20 marks)

Answer question **1** and either question **2** or question **3**.

Norman MacCaig is one of the foremost Scottish poets of the twentieth century. In this poem he records his impressions of New York during his first visit there. He is particularly moved by his experience of the city at night.

Read the poem at least twice and then respond to the questions following it.

HOTEL ROOM 12TH FLOOR

This morning I watched from here
a helicopter skirting like a damaged insect
the Empire State Building, that
jumbo size dentist's drill, and landing
on the roof of the PanAm skyscraper.   5
But now midnight has come in
from foreign places. Its uncivilised darkness
is shot at by a million lit windows, all
ups and acrosses.

But midnight is not   10
so easily defeated. I lie in bed, between
a radio and a television set, and hear
the wildest of warwhoops continually ululating through
the glittering canyons and gulches —
police cars and ambulances racing   15
to broken bones, the harsh screaming
from coldwater flats, the blood
glazed on sidewalks.

The frontier is never
somewhere else. And no stockades   20
can keep the midnight out.

                                    Norman MacCaig

1.   What does this poem say to you about the city? Point out the words or phrases that especially convey
      its message to you.   (10)

Answer 2 or 3

2.   The poet uses the word "midnight" three times in the poem. In the overall context of the poem what
      do you think he means by the word midnight?   (10)

OR

3.   What impresses you about this poem? Quote from or refer to the text in support of your opinion.
                                                                                         (10)

B. PRESCRIBED POETRY (50 marks)

Candidates must answer **one** of the following questions (**1 — 4**).

1. "Emily Dickinson's poems are an intense personal account of her celebrations and her despairs."

   Discuss this view of the poems of Emily Dickinson on your course. Support your discussion by quotation from or reference to the poems you have studied.

2. "The subjects of Heaney's poems are treated with great love and sympathy together with a keen eye for significant detail."

   Would you agree with this estimation of the poems by Seamus Heaney on your course? Support your point of view by relevant quotation or reference.

3. Write a short essay on the aspects of Michael Longley's poems (their content **and/or** style) that you found most interesting. Support your discussion by reference to or quotation from the poems you have studied.

4. "Shakespeare's sonnets are lively reflections on Love and Time."

   How true is this statement of the Shakespearean sonnets you have studied? Support your discussion by reference to or quotation from the poems.

English – Higher Level – Paper I

SAMPLE PAPER 1

Total Marks: 200

Time: 2¹/₂ hours

- This paper is divided into two sections,
  Section I COMPREHENDING and Section II COMPOSING.
- The paper contains **four** texts on the general theme of READERS and WRITERS.
- Candidates should familiarise themselves with each of the texts before beginning their answers.

- Both sections of this paper (Comprehending and Composing) must be attempted.
- Each section carries 100 marks.

SECTION I – COMPREHENDING

- Two questions, A and B, follow each text.
- Candidates must answer a Question A on one text and a Question B on a different text. Candidates must answer only one Question A and only one Question B.
- **N.B.** Candidates may NOT answer a Question A and a Question B on the same text.

SECTION II – COMPOSING

Candidates must write on **one** of the compositions 1–7.

Sample 1

SECTION I
COMPREHENDING (100 marks)

TEXT 1
A Soldier's Declaration

Siegfried Sassoon was one of the great poets of World War 1. He was awarded the Military Cross for,
"conspicuous gallantry during a raid. He remained for one and a half hours under rifle and bomb
fire collecting and bringing in our wounded. Owing to his courage and determination, all the killed
and wounded were brought in."
As the war dragged on, however, Sassoon became more and more angry at the wasteful loss of life
and what the soldiers had to endure in the trenches. His moral courage was equal to his physical
bravery. He was the first to publicly accuse the authorities of sacrificing men's lives by prolonging
the war. This public denunciation was published in July 1917 to the consternation of the military
authorities.

I am making this statement as an act of wilful defiance of military authority, because I believe the war is being deliberately prolonged by those who have the power to end it.

I am a soldier, convinced that I am acting on behalf of soldiers. I believe that this war, upon which I entered as a war of defence and liberation, has now become a war of aggression and conquest. I believe that the purposes for which I and my fellow soldiers entered upon this war should have been so clearly stated as to have made it impossible to change them, and that, had this been done, the objects which actuated us would now be attainable by negotiation.

I have seen and endured the suffering of the troops, and I can no longer be a party to prolong these sufferings for ends which I believe to be evil and unjust.

I am not protesting against the conduct of the war, but against the political errors and insincerities for which the fighting men are being sacrificed.

On behalf of those who are suffering now I make this protest against the deception which is being practised on them; also I believe that I may help to destroy the callous complacence with which the majority of those at home regard the continuance of agonies which they do not share, and which they have not sufficient imagination to realize.

(235 words)

N.B. Candidates may NOT answer Question A and Question B on the same text.
Questions A and B carry 50 marks each.

Question A

(i) The writer begins by stating that his declaration is in "defiance of military authority". Show how he goes on to develop that statement in the course of the passage. (25)

(ii) Do you think that this passage would persuade readers that the writer's protest is sincere and justified? Give reasons for your answer. (25)

Question B

Write a persuasive passage for publication in a newspaper, protesting against something that you regard as wrong or unjust at the present time. (50)

TEXT 2
Childhood Reading

In the following passage, Seamus Heaney recalls his earliest experiences of reading at home and looks back on the comic characters that fascinated and entertained him.

When I was learning to read, towards the end of 1945, the most important books in the house were the ration books – the pink clothes coupons and the green 'points' for sweets and groceries. There wasn't much reading done apart from the deaths column of the *Irish Weekly* and the auctions page of the *Northern Constitution*. 'I am instructed by the representatives of the late John James Halferty, Drumanee ...' My father lay on the sofa and rehearsed the acres, roods and perches of arable and meadow land in a formal tone and with a certain enlargement of the spirit.

On a shelf, behind a screen and too high to be reached anyhow, there were four or five mouldering volumes that may have belonged to my Aunt Susan from her days in Orange's Academy, but they remained closed books to me. The first glimpse I have of myself reading on my own is one of those orphaned memories, a moment without context that will always stay with me. It is a book from the school library – a padlocked box that was opened more or less as a favour – involving explorers in cork helmets and 'savages', with illustrations of war canoes on a jungle river. The oil lamp is lit and a neighbour called Hugh Bates is interrupting me. 'Boys but this Seamus fellow is a great scholar. What book are you in now, son?' And my father is likely wringing what he can from the moment with 'He's as bad as Pat McGuckin this minute.'

contd →

Pat McGuckin was a notorious bachelor farmer – a cousin of ours – who was said to burn his scone like King Alfred every time he lifted a book. Years later, when *Death of a Naturalist* was published, the greatest commendation at home was 'Lord knows Pat would fairly have enjoyed this.'

Of course, there were always religious magazines like the *Far East* and the *Messenger* – Pudsy Ryan in the children's corner of the former was the grown-ups' idea of a side-splitting turn, but even then I found his mis-spellings a bit heavy-handed. Far better were the technicolour splendours of Korky the Cat and Big Eggo in the *Dandy* and *Beano*. The front pages of these comics opened like magic casements on Desperate Dan, Lord Snooty, Hungry Horace, Keyhole Kate, Julius Sneezer and Jimmy and his Magic Patch and probably constituted my first sense of the invitations of fiction. They were passed round at school, usually fairly tattered, but every now and again my mother brought a new one from Castledawson, without a fold in it, its primary colours blazing with excitements to come. Occasionally, also, an American comic – all colour from beginning to end – arrived from the American airbase nearby, with Li'l Abner, Ferdinand and Blondie speaking a language that even Pat McGuckin did not know.

There was a resistance to buying new comics in our house, not out of any educational nicety, but because of a combination of two attitudes: that they were a catch-penny and that somehow they were the thin end of the wedge, that if you let them into the house then next step was the *Empire News, Thompson's Weekly, Tit-Bits* and the *News of the World*. Nevertheless, I ended up persuading my mother to place a regular order for the *Champion*, a higher-class comic altogether, featuring a Biggles-rides-again figure called Rockfist Rogan and Ginger Nutt ('the boy who takes the *bis-cake*', in South Derry parlance) and Colwyn Dane, the sleuth. With the *Champion* I entered the barter market for the *Rover*, the *Hotspur*, the *Wizard* and any other pulp the presses of old England could deliver. I skimmed through all those 'ain'ts' and 'cors' and 'yoicks' and 'blimeys', and skimmed away contented.

(634 words)

N.B. Candidates may NOT answer Question A and Question B on the same text.
Questions A and B carry 50 marks each.

Question A

(i)   Outline what you learn about the Heaney household, their way of life and the area in which they lived in this passage. (20)

(ii) From your reading of the piece, would you say that memories are very important to this writer? Explain your answer. (20)

(iii) What do you think was the attraction of these comics for the young Heaney? (15)

Question B

Take some well known figure from the world of entertainment or politics and write an extract from his or her autobiography (150–200 words), suggesting the books or reading material you think you would find in his or her childhood memories. (50)

TEXT 3 — Catherine Cookson

In this introduction to a 1999 biography of the popular novelist, Catherine Cookson, the biographer speaks about literacy in the late nineteenth and early twentieth century. Far from being considered a natural right, it was discouraged in the lower classes as something dangerous to the social order which kept the poor in their place. This fear of the power of literacy is reflected in the novels of Catherine Cookson. The passage also makes the point that a lack of written family records makes the biographer's work difficult.

Literacy on the lower side of the upstairs/downstairs divide was actually discouraged. When the introduction of free education for everyone was debated Parliament, there were many who feared that education would only foment social unrest and could even lead to industrial and economic decline. Theresa Rosier, the young edcationalist in Catherine Cookson's novel *Katie Mulholland*, is discouraged from organising classes for working men and told by her parents, 'Child, do you think a miner would go down a mine if he could read and write correctly? Do you want your father's business to collapse? Do you want us to starve?' It also drove a wedge between neighbours. Those who wanted to better themselves were considered upstarts and treated with suspicion. Catherine Cookson describes the dilemma in her novel *The Black Velvet Gown*. Her heroine, Riah, living in a nineteenth-century northeastern community, is unusual because she has been taught to read and write by her husband. She is proud of the fact that her children are the only ones in the three rows of pit houses who can write their names. 'This alone had set them apart. Seth could have taught lots of men in the rows to read and write, but they were afraid in case the pit keeker split on them to the manager, because reading was frowned upon, and, as some of the older men had pointed out forcibly to Seth, it got you nowhere except in trouble with those that provided your livelihood.' Not only did education make them unpopular with their employers, it did nothing to improve their social conditions. As Catherine has one of her characters remark in *The Mallen Litter*, 'What are they after, them up there, eh, forcin' them to school? You can't fill their bellies with readin' an' writin'.'

In the first two decades of the twentieth century, despite the introduction of free, compulsory education up to the age of thirteen in 1880, adult literacy was still a big problem among the working classes. Most adults over thirty had grown up in families too poor to afford much in the way of schooling, and where earning a living took priority over education. Catherine Cookson's family, the McMullens, were no exception. The man who brought her up, her step-grandfather John McMullen, born in the 1850s, could not even sign his name. He collected his pension by putting a thumb print on the form. His wife Rose, Catherine's grandmother, could read but found writing a letter arduous. Her daughters Sarah, Kate and Mary had received rather more in the way of education, but were all working by the time they were twelve. They could read and write, but only at a fairly basic level.

The McMullen clan lived closely together. They rarely needed to write letters to each other, or to anyone else, and they didn't have the time or the privacy to keep diaries. Like millions of other working-class families, they left little record of their existence or the details of their daily lives and when they died they were buried in unmarked graves. If little Katie McMullen had not grown up to become a best-selling novelist, we would know nothing about them at all. The problem for the biographer is how to chronicle such invisible lives.

(552 words)

N.B. Candidates may NOT answer Question A and Question B on the same text.

Questions A and B carry 50 marks each.

Question A

(i) In her opening paragraph, the writer deals with the historical and social issue of literacy. Explain how in that paragraph, she relates this general issue to the subject of her biography. (10)

(ii) From the extracts cited, what impression of the fictional world of Catherine Cookson do you have from your reading of this passage? (10)

(iii) According to the writer, why was "adult literacy still a problem" in the first two decades of the twentieth century? Explain how she illustrates this problem in the lives of the McMullen family. (20)

(iv) Would your reading of this introduction encourage you to read the biography? Give reasons for your answer. (20)

Question B

Write an introduction to a literary biography in which you argue that learning about a writer's life is an important part of understanding his or her work. (200 words approx) (50)

TEXT 4
Segregated Teaching

Carolyn Forche is an American poet who has won many awards both for her poetry and for her international activities for human rights. She has worked as a correspondent in Beirut, Lebanon, South Africa and El Salvador. Many of her poems describe atrocities and oppression suffered by writers in some of the worst political regimes of the twentieth century.

In the passage below, she describes one of her first teaching jobs when she was twenty-four and very unsure about how to handle a difficult situation. She was guided by her own best instincts and tried to lead the group into a better belief in themselves and the value of their own experience.

On the first day of my first semester of teaching in 1974 and without any pedagogical preparation, I found myself before a classroom of what were euphemistically called "remedial" writing students. They were mostly minority students, who had been bussed to rural, white Bowling Green University from the ghettoes of Chicago and Detroit, under various programs designed to "integrate" the student body. The policy was called "open admissions." Anyone with a high school diploma or its equivalent could enter the university, according to liberal principles of equal opportunity. The students were given attractive financial aid packages. What they were *not* given were the skills to remain academically viable. Most of them had passed through high school without acquiring the ability to read or write standard English. I was to teach them the rudiments of essay writing, and at the end of my three months, was to have prepared them to pass a university-wide examination in composition and rhetoric. I was given a list of "suggested texts" which I thought highly of, except

that my students couldn't *read* them. To make matters worse, I found myself before a racially self-segregated classroom of poor inner-city African-Americans and poor rural whites. An empty row of desks between the two groups served as a no-man's land. This was not an auspicious beginning.

I didn't know quite what to do, so I announced to the class that I simply couldn't teach in a segregated classroom, and proposed that I leave for ten minutes while they discussed possible solutions. When I returned to class, the no-man's land was a bit more populated, and the class was involved in a rather heated discussion about whose fault the segregation had been. I assigned them to write a narrative about their childhoods in their own words and in their own hand, assuring them that I wouldn't assign grades to these papers. The next day, I asked them to read their papers aloud. They weren't called upon, and so we endured many long silences between volunteers.

contd →

The narratives were poorly written, but they were compelling and interesting and provoked an unexpected reaction of shock among these students at the similarities between the childhoods of the African-American and white rural poor. Affected by each other's stories, they slowly allied themselves. I confessed to them that their teacher was a rank beginner, but that I cared about their success, and in exchange for their assistance in "training" me, I would certainly dedicate myself to helping them stay in school.

It took me two weeks to persuade them that the mastery of standard English was necessary. I divided them into small, integrated "affinity groups," believing that they would be more comfortable reading their work to a few rather than many peers. The stronger students in each group became tutors for the others. I devoted long hours to high-speed grammar games. Without knowing yet about "process" writing, I encouraged them to think of each paper as a draft toward a paper. Papers could be revised again and again until they were worthy of a passing, or even a high grade.

I did lose a few students: one to drug dependency, another to mysterious and compelling circumstances at home. On the day of the examination, I gave them a pep talk, but also announced that perhaps some of them would fail the exam. As it happened, most already knew this, but didn't feel particularly fearful or saddened. They would come back, they said, and try again. To my surprise and delight, three-quarters of the class passed. When the scores were posted, they invited me to their party. Even the students who failed the exam were there. They wanted to celebrate and to inform their teacher that she had "passed". I knew then – I must have known – that I had stumbled into an honored and loved profession unwittingly. Shortly thereafter, I received notice that I would be teaching the advanced composition students from then on, according to the mysterious logic of the educational bureaucracy, who believed they were rewarding me for my success with the poorest students.

(656 words)

N.B. Candidates may NOT answer Question A and Question B on the same text.
Questions A and B carry 50 marks each.

Question A

(i) In the opening paragraph what difficulties does the writer say she faced in this teaching assignment? (10)

(ii) Describe her strategy in confronting the problem of the segregated classroom and give your views on this strategy. (10)

(iii) She uses the terms "affinity groups" and "process" writing. From your reading of the text what is your understanding of these two terms? (10)

(iv) Reread the closing paragraph, describing the writer's feelings about this experience and the tone in which she conveys those feelings to the reader. (20)

Question B

Write a report by Carolyn Forche's teaching supervisor in which you give an account of her task and assess the way in which she handled it. (50)

SECTION II
COMPOSING (100 marks)

Write a composition on **any one** of the following.
Each composition carries 100 marks.

The composition assignments below are intended to reflect language study in the areas of information, argument, persuasion, narration and the aesthetic use of language.

1. "I have seen and endured the suffering of the troops." (TEXT 1)

   Write an informative report, from an officer on active military service, complaining about conditions on the battlefront and demanding action from the authorities to relieve the situation.

2. "A padlocked box that was opened more or less as a favour." (TEXT 2)

   Compose a series of diary entries in which you and a parent spend some days in the home of a deceased relative, finding old papers and possessions from that person's life.

3. "The Black Velvet Gown" (TEXT 3)

   Imagine you are a writer of historical fiction. Compose an episode in which this phrase figures.

4. "What book are you in now, son?" (TEXT 2)

   Write an address for a school parents' evening in which you persuade parents of the importance of encouraging their children to read in their leisure time at home.

5. "The problem for the biographer is how to chronicle such invisible lives." (TEXT 3)

   Write a short story inspired by the phrase *Invisible Lives*.

6. "There was a resistance to buying new comics in our house." (TEXT 2)

   Seamus Heaney is writing about Ireland in the forties and describing the comics on sale for children at that time. Argue the case for buying or not buying the popular comics and magazines that are available to children in Ireland today.

7. **Write an article, intended for publication in your local newspaper, outlining the difficulties faced by adults with literacy problems.**

LEAVING CERTIFICATE EXAMINATION

English – Higher Level – Paper 2

SAMPLE PAPER 1

Total Marks: 200

Time: 3 hours 20 minutes

Candidates must attempt the following:

- **ONE** question in SECTION I – The Single Text
- **ONE** question from SECTION II – The Comparative Study
- **ONE** question on the Unseen Poem from SECTION III – Poetry
- **ONE** question on Prescribed Poetry from SECTION III – Poetry

N.B. Candidates must answer on Shakespearean Drama.
They may do so in SECTION I, The Single Text *(King Lear)*
OR in SECTION II, The Comparative Study *(King Lear, The Tempest)*

INDEX OF SINGLE TEXTS

Sample 1

SECTION I

SINGLE TEXT (60 MARKS)

Candidates must answer **one** question from this section (A–E).

A   WUTHERING HEIGHTS — Emily Brontë

  (i)   The voice of the Narrator is central to the novel *Wuthering Heights*.'

      Write a response to this statement, supporting your ideas by reference to the text.

OR

  (ii) 'Catherine Earnshaw was a victim of her own wilfullness.'

      Discuss this assessment of her character, supporting your answer with reference to the novel.

B   DANCING AT LUGHNASA — Brian Friel

  (i)   From your study of *Dancing at Lughnasa*, would you agree that 'Brian Friel is Ireland's greatest playwright'?

      Discuss this statement with suitable reference to the text.

OR

  (ii) 'The themes of Love and Religion are at the heart of Friel's play *Dancing at Lughnasa*.'

      Discuss this view, supporting your answer with reference to the text.

C KING LEAR — William Shakespeare

(i) Discuss the view that *King Lear* explores the struggle between Good and Evil.

Support your answer with close reference to the text.

OR

(ii) 'Despite his poor judgement at the start, Lear finally earns our respect and admiration.' Discuss the character of Lear in the light of this statement.

D THE GRAPES OF WRATH — John Steinbeck

(i) Write a detailed review of Steinbeck's classic novel, *The Grapes of Wrath*. Include in your answer an evaluation of Characters, Themes and Style.

OR

(ii) 'Tom Joad is a man of heroic stature.'

Discuss this view of the main character in *The Grapes of Wrath*, supporting your answer with suitable reference to the novel.

E THE BLACKWATER LIGHTSHIP — Colm Tóibín

(i) Write a letter to the author, Colm Tóibín, outlining the impact the novel had on you. Support your answer with suitable reference.

OR

(ii) 'Declan's suffering has managed to reconcile the conflicts as well as strengthen the bonds within his family.'

Respond to this statement with reference to the novel *The Blackwater Lightship*.

SECTION II

COMPARATIVE STUDY (70 MARKS)

Candidates must answer **one** question from **either A – Literary Genre or B** – The General Vision and Viewpoint.

In your answer you may not use the text you have answered on in **Section I** – The Single Text.

N.B. The questions use the word **text** to refer to all the different kinds of texts available for study on this course, i.e. novel, play, short story, autobiography, biography, travel writing and film. The questions use the word **author** to refer to novelists, playwrights, writers in all genres, and film directors.

A LITERARY GENRE

1. 'Key moments in a text can reveal the craftsmanship of the author.'

    (a) Show how this statement applies to **one** of the texts on your comparative course.
    (70 marks)

    (b) Compare how key moments in **two other texts** highlight the artistry of the authors.
    (40 marks)

OR

2. 'The Art of Storytelling is unique to each author.'

    Compare **at least two texts** from your comparative course in the light of this statement.
    (70 marks)

B THE GENERAL VISION AND VIEWPOINT

1. 'Each text will present us with its own general vision and viewpoint.'

    (a) Write a note on the general vision and viewpoint of **one** of the texts you have studied for your comparative course.
    (30 marks)

    (b) Compare **two other texts** you have studied in the light of this statement.
    (40 marks)

OR

2. 'The author's vision and viewpoint form the backdrop to our appreciation of a text.'

    In the light of this statement, compare the general vision and viewpoint in the texts you have studied for your comparative course.
    (70 marks)

SECTION III

POETRY (70 MARKS)

Candidates must answer **A** – Unseen Poem **and B** – Prescribed Poetry.

A   UNSEEN POEM (20 Marks)

Answer **either** Question **1** or Question **2**.

In this poem, a father talks to his son about how best to live life. On the one hand, he suggests living for the day; on the other, planning wisely for the future. Clearly, the advice given is not simply about gardening and food. Look for the concerns here about different needs in life.

Advice to My Son

The trick is, to live your days
as if each one may be your last
(for they go fast, and young men lose their lives
in strange and unimaginable ways)
but at the same time, plan long range
(for they go slow: if you survive
the shattered windshield and the bursting shell
you will arrive
at our approximation here below
of heaven or hell).

To be specific, between the peony and the rose
plant squash and spinach, turnips and tomatoes;
beauty is nectar
and nectar, in a desert, saves –
but the stomach craves stronger sustenance
than the honied vine.

Therefore, marry a pretty girl
after seeing her mother;
show your soul to one man, work with another;
and always serve bread with your wine.

But, son,
always serve wine.

Peter Meinke

1.   What advice is this father giving his son about plants in the second stanza?
     What do you think are the father's real concerns in giving this advice?   (20 marks)

OR

2.   Choose two lines from the poem (these may or may not be consecutive)
     which you found especially striking and comment upon their impact
     on the reader.   (20 marks)

B PRESCRIBED POETRY (50 marks)

Candidates must answer **one** of the following questions (**1 – 4**).

1. **Eavan Boland**
   'Boland's poetry revolves around a world with which we can all identify.'

   Respond to this statement, referring to the poems of Eavan Boland that you have studied.

2. **Patrick Kavanagh**
   Write a personal response to the poetry of Patrick Kavanagh.

3. **Michael Longley**
   'Longley's poetry deals with many important themes and issues.'

   Discuss this statement in the light of the poetry of Michael Longley. Support your answer with suitable quotations.

4. **Derek Walcott**
   'Walcott's poetry is refreshingly original.'

   Write out a presentation you would give to your classmates under the above heading, referring to the poetry of Derek Walcott that you have studied.

LEAVING CERTIFICATE EXAMINATION

English – Higher Level – Paper I

SAMPLE PAPER 2

Total Marks: 200

Time: 2¹/₂ hours

- This paper is divided into two sections,
  Section I COMPREHENDING and Section II COMPOSING.
- The paper contains **four** texts on the general theme of FASHION and
  THE MEDIA.
- Candidates should familiarise themselves with each of the texts before
  beginning their answers.

- Both sections of this paper (Comprehending and Composing) must be
  attempted.
- Each section carries 100 marks.

SECTION I – COMPREHENDING

- Two questions, A and B, follow each text.
- Candidates must answer a Question A on one text and a Question B on a
  different text. Candidates must answer only one Question A and only one
  Question B.
- **N.B.** Candidates may NOT answer a Question A and a Question B on the
  same text..

SECTION II – COMPOSING

Candidates must write on **one** of the compositions 1–7.

SECTION I
COMPREHENDING (100 marks)

TEXT 1 — Breakfast Television

In the following article, published in *The Listener*, the writer and broadcaster, Ludovic Kennedy comments on a breakfast television show and gives his opinions on the content and personalities involved.

Hello, good morning and welcome to the Mission to Explain Show.

This is Mike. Mike's nice. Mike has ginger hair and a ginger moustache and looks like the rugger master at a boys' prep school. Mike used to have a colleague called Nick who looked like a Wimbledon ticket tout, but he hasn't been around for a while.

This is Anne. Anne's pretty. Anne used to have lovely black hair, but it's mostly ginger now to match Mike's moustache. She scratches it a lot (everything OK there, Anne?). Anne looks like a super-cool, super-efficient chairman's right-hand girl. Sometimes Kathy takes Anne's place. Kathy has lovely dark hair like Anne used to have and is just as pretty and doesn't make so many faces.

You can't help but admire the relaxed, spontaneous way Mike and Anne interview people, even the thickest, though they do have an odd trick of glancing at the camera from time to time, as if to make quite sure we're still there.

Mike and Anne use a language which is all their own. The other day Anne asked a man called Hank whether Rock and Roll wasn't a 'faded art form', while on National Courtesy Day Mike told us, 'Politeness is our birthright.' Over on *Breakfast Time* they tell different things in the same tone of voice, but on the Mission to Explain Show when something solemn comes up they have to stop giggling and start being po-faced.

And they say things to match. The day after the Greek cruise liner had sunk Anne said, 'Of course, all our thoughts are very much with the families of those that are still missing.' Well, mine weren't, Anne, and I doubt if yours were either, but that's the kind of yuk the feeble-minded like to hear, right?

'Of course' is one of Anne's favourite phrases. Joan Collins would be there next day, she said, to tell us why she had dedicated her book to her father 'who, of course, died last year'. For Christ's sake, Anne, some of us didn't even know that Joan Collins *had* a father. I shall miss Anne, now she's gone. Hurry back.

Mike's euphemisms are modelled on those of Charlie Chester. The other day he told us he wanted to 'pay tribute' to someone who had 'passed over at age sixty-four'. Mike, he didn't pass over or through or up or anywhere. He *died*. Mike also spoke recently of 'a hero of considerable proportions' as if he were a Michelin man.

This is Carol, who does the weather and looks like a small, plump blackbird. Standing by a map that must have been drawn by a five-year-old, she gabbles away at such a rate that you are lucky to pick up more than about one word in ten. Fewer teeth might help. Sometimes Carol says, 'Hello, and nice to see you,' but as all she is looking at is a piece of hardware, she probably means 'Hello, and nice for you to see me.'

This is Gyles, who gives the impression he's wandered on to the wrong channel – he is wearing a yellow golf ball on his sweater and looks quite demented. Gyles tells us of a boy who can hold 272 marbles in his trouser pocket and that a rat can go longer without water than a camel. He also brings us a knock, knock story. 'Dishwater.' 'Dishwater what?' 'Dishwater way I used to speak before I got false teeth.' That's the fun of the Mission to Explain Show – you never know what's going to turn up.

(380 words)

N.B. Candidates may NOT answer Question A and Question B on the same text.
Questions A and B carry 50 marks each.

Question A

(i) What are this writer's feelings towards both the show and the personalities he is describing in this article? (10)

(ii) Explain how the language he uses expresses those feelings. (10)

(iii) The writer criticises the way in which the television personalities use the English language. What does he dislike about their use of English? (10)

(iv) Did you enjoy reading this article? Give reasons for your answer. (20)

Question B

Write an article for a television or radio magazine in which you give your commentary on a morning programme. Your article will be published in a magazine for viewers and listeners which has a wide mass audience. (50)

TEXT 2

A Fashion Photograph

The following photograph is taken from the front cover of a magazine colour supplement.

N.B. Candidates may NOT answer Question A and Question B on the same text.
Questions A and B carry 50 marks each.

Question A

(i) Describe the face, clothes, accessories and gesture of the woman in this photograph. (10)

(ii) What lifestyle is suggested by the image as a whole? (10)

(iii) How is this lifestyle suggested? (10)

(iv) Write the article (about 200 words) which you think the magazine editor would place alongside this photograph. (20)

Question B

Choosing as your heading, **either** WEDDINGS **or** TRAVEL, write an article for a glossy, expensive magazine aimed at affluent, fashion-conscious readers. (50)

Clare Boylan's
Breakfast Venue of the Month

Powerscourt Estate
Enniskerry, Co Wicklow

You won't find a Leinster Fry nor even devilled kidneys under silver domes at this converted stately home but you can literally dine like a lord on the terrace of the light and airy restaurant, directly overlooking the magnificent Italianate gardens which were once the back yard of Lord and Lady Powerscourt. For those who believe location is everything, then this al fresco breakfast venue offers one of the very best views of Ireland. As you sip your (excellent) coffee and bask in the last of the summer sun, you can admire the formal terraces with their statues and terraces and topiary and fountain backed by the Sugarloaf mountain.

Breakfast is a particularly good time to visit Powerscourt as you can have the stately demesne to yourself before the coaches start rolling up for lunch. The food is light but good. There is excellent coffee (filter or cappuccino). A wide range of teas includes Earl Grey, fruit teas and infusions. Commendably, there is also a filtered water machine and a constant supply of ice. Bread is home-made and the selection includes wholemeal, apricot, walnut and raisin and a delicious cheese bread. When we arrived at 10am the bread was still being baked. There were however, muffins, scones, banana and walnut bread, carrot cake, giant ginger and chocolate chip cookies and a diet-busting array of tarts and cakes. My companion felt like something fruity and settled for a salad which included melon, strawberry, fresh peach, cucumber and mint. The flavour was excellent but the salad had a slightly settled air. A large mug of filter coffee and a frothy cappuccino were both as good as it gets. We both adored the banana and walnut bread, which came as a mini loaf with icing and a pecan nut on top. A crumbly fruit scone with home made raspberry jam and whipped cream drew no complaints. Last year's car-parking charge of £2 per vehicle has now been abolished and our noble repast brought a very modest breakfast bill of £7.

The breakfast menu would be greatly enhanced by the simple addition of a fruit compote, some Greek yogurt and honey and some nice crunchy little croissants and the service could have been a good deal more enthusiastic. But even without these refinements it is rapidly getting to be a favourite Saturday morning spot. And as the weekend stretches out ahead of you, there is plenty of time for a walk in the beautiful gardens or along the banks of the Dargle River.

Tropicana breakfast rating: 4 out of 5.

(420 words)

N.B. Candidates may NOT answer Question A and Question B on the same text.
Questions A and B carry 50 marks each.

Question A

(i) This passage is taken from a popular magazine. What do you think is its purpose? (10)

(ii) Magazine writers must engage and hold the attention of the reader in the opening paragraph.
Do you think the opening paragraph here is a successful beginning in this context? (10)

(iii) In the remaining paragraphs, do you think the writer presents her subject well? Give reasons for your answer. (20)

(iv) What is the purpose of the visuals which accompany the text? (10)

Question B

Write a restaurant review for a publication of your choice. Briefly introduce your review, explaining the kind of publication for which you intend it. (50)

Fashion

In this article, Nancy Etcoff outlines her views on fashion and what it reveals about the wearer.

Fashion is an art form, a status marker and a display of attitude. We create it, as we create architecture and furniture, to help us negotiate our relations with the outside world and to provide us with comfort and protection. But, as visual extensions of our person, they also mirror our desires in complex ways.

Fashion is of the moment. The most expensive clothing makes its debut in a setting of live theatre: months of work culminate in a brief, dazzling display before an invited audience. Great clothes are all about making a drop-dead entrance. Contemporary fashions may allude to the faraway but they are always about the here and now, about seizing the moment and searing it into memory.

Fashion may chatter about many things but the conversation is mainly about sex and status.

British designer Katherine Hamnett: "Fashion is all about mating ... Think about an 18-year-old ... that energy to try on 20 different t-shirts before going out – to them it is so important ..." "True fashion obsession is something to do with sex," says Gucci designer, Tom Ford. We use fashion to make us look younger, taller, richer, to appear unblemished and unwearied.

However, sex is only part of the fashion story. A fashion that is in one season and out the next shows what pure status effects look like. Stripped of social meaning, the garment looks worthless, even ridiculous. Competition may drive fashion to excess and ignite fashion crazes but the pursuit is not frivolous or silly. The game may be frenzied but the players are operating rationally. They know clothes are valuable currency in the social arena. They show we are ahead of the pack or, at the very least, not left behind.

Clothes must also give evidence of *conspicuous leisure*. By leisure, economist Thorstein Veblen meant enjoying activities not involved in making money or producing anything useful. Clothing often reflects high-status pastimes like hunting, golf, yachting or polo.

contd →

Sample 2

The riding coat and hat from the English hunter were the inspiration for the top hat and tails of evening wear, the brass buttons and blazer of the yachting world became acceptable sportswear on land, the cardigan sweater and the polo shirt migrated from the playing field to the home. Today we have what has been dubbed "patagonia couture", clothing derived from scuba diving or snowboarding or mountain climbing.

Another way to convey that one leads a life of leisure is to wear fabrics requiring high maintenance. A good example is linen, because it is a high prestige fabric that wrinkles the moment you put it on. The satin brocade and embroidered shoes of the 17th century French aristocracy showed their women never walked in mud. They did not have to: their sedans were brought directly into public rooms at Versailles. Today's diaphanous slip dresses do not look as if they could stand up to any challenge at all.

Leisure is most obviously displayed by fashions that make labour impossible. Chinese aristocrats wore long fingernails to show they did not perform manual labour. As a recent fashion reporter noted: "High heels are for those who pay other people to do their walking for them – to the dry cleaner, to fetch a cab, to pick up lunch."

(530 words)

N.B. Candidates may NOT answer Question A and Question B on the same text.
Questions A and B carry 50 marks each.

Question A

(i) Outline accurately and concisely the author's illustration of her opening statement; "Fashion is an art form, a status marker and a display of attitude". (15)

(ii) The writer believes that our choice of clothing tells an intelligent observer a great deal about us. Do you agree with this view? Give reasons for your answer. (15)

(iii) What connections does she make between leisure and clothing? (20)

Question B

Write an address to your class in which you argue for or against the case that fashion plays too great a role in the lives of the young. (50)

SECTION II
COMPOSING   (100 marks)

Write a composition on **any one** of the following.
Each composition carries 100 marks.

The composition assignments below are intended to reflect language study in the areas of information, argument, persuasion, narration and the aesthetic use of language.

1. "When something solemn comes up they have to stop giggling and start being po-faced." (TEXT 1)

    Write an article for a popular magazine in which you argue the case that there is a low standard of journalism on many popular television or radio programmes.

2. As a recent fashion reporter noted: "High heels are for those who pay other people to do their walking for them – to the dry-cleaners, to fetch a cab, to pick up lunch." (TEXT 4)

    Write a script, intended for broadcast on a radio programme on world poverty, arguing the case that the gap between those who live luxuriously and those who struggle to exist has become unacceptably wide.

3. **Compose a narrative inspired by TEXT 2.**

4. **Write a features passage for a newspaper in which you give an account of a social event attended by the woman in TEXT 2.**

5. "Clothes are valuable currency in the social arena." (TEXT 4)

    Write a publicity brochure in which you persuade aspiring politicians or celebrities to take a course in your newly-formed company. Your course offers training in how to dress well for public life and television appearances.

6. "... directly overlooking the magnificent Italianate gardens which were once the back yard of Lord and Lady Powerscourt."

    Write the opening of a historical novel which tells the story of a family living in a Great House of a past century.

7. **Write an article, intended for publication in a school magazine, in which you outline your views on breakfast television.**

LEAVING CERTIFICATE EXAMINATION

English – Higher Level – Paper 2

SAMPLE PAPER 2

Total Marks: 200

Time: 3 hours 20 minutes

Candidates must attempt the following:

- **ONE** question in SECTION I – The Single Text
- **ONE** question from SECTION II – The Comparative Study
- **ONE QUESTION** on the Unseen Poem from SECTION III – Poetry
- **ONE** question on Prescribed Poetry from SECTION III – Poetry

N.B. Candidates must answer on Shakespearean Drama.
They may do so in SECTION I, The Single Text (*King Lear*)
OR in SECTION II, The Comparative Study (*King Lear, The Tempest*).

INDEX OF SINGLE TEXTS

SECTION I

SINGLE TEXT (60 marks)

Candidates must answer **one** question from this section (A–E).

A WUTHERING HEIGHTS — Emily Brontë

(i) 'Despite all his fiendish traits, we still manage to maintain a certain admiration for Heathcliff.'

To what extent would you agree with this view of the novel? Support your answer with suitable reference to the text.

OR

(ii) Discuss the view that the novel *Wuthering Heights* depicts a world of stark contrasts.

Support your answer with suitable reference to the text.

B DANCING AT LUGHNASA — Brian Friel

(i) Write a detailed review for a national newspaper of the drama *Dancing at Lughnasa*. Your review should include an evaluation of Plot, Characters and Themes.

OR

(ii) 'The Mundy sisters give us a unique insight into the complexities of family life.'

Write a response to the above statement, supporting your answer with close reference to the play.

C   KING LEAR — William Shakespeare

(i)   'Cordelia's stubborn pride throughout the "Love Test" brings about the tragedy within the play.'

To what extent do you agree with this assessment of Shakespeare's play? Support your points with suitable reference and quotation.

OR

(ii)   'The genius of William Shakespeare is self-evident in his tragedy *King Lear*.'

Discuss this view of the play, supporting your answer with suitable reference.

D   THE GRAPES OF WRATH — John Steinbeck

(i)   'The Great Depression of the 1930s forms the context for the poverty and misfortune of Steinbeck's novel.'

Write a response to the above statement, supporting your answer with suitable reference to *The Grapes of Wrath*.

OR

Discuss the view that Steinbeck's novel *The Grapes of Wrath* is predominantly concerned with the theme of Family.

Support your answer with reference to the text.

E   THE BLACKWATER LIGHTSHIP — Colm Tóibín

(i)   'Change, both personally and in society, is a major concern of the novel.'

Respond to this statement, supporting your answer with suitable reference to Tóibín's novel *The Blackwater Lightship*.

OR

(ii)   'The character of Helen and her narrative voice dominate the novel *The Blackwater Lightship*.'

Discuss with suitable reference to the text.

SECTION II

COMPARATIVE STUDY (70 marks)

Candidates must answer **one** question from **either A** – The Cultural Context **or B** – The General Vision and Viewpoint.

In your answer you may not use the text you have answered on in **Section I** – The Single Text.

N.B. The questions use the word **text** to refer to all the different kinds of texts available for study on this course, i.e. novel, play, short story, autobiography, biography, travel writing and film. The questions use the word **author** to refer to novelists, playwrights, writers in all genres, and film directors.

A THE CULTURAL CONTEXT

1. 'The values of a particular society will be revealed in the key moments of a text.'
   (a) In the case of **one** comparative text you have studied, give a detailed account of at least one key moment in the light of the above statement.   (30 marks)
   (b) Compare the key moments from **two other** texts you have studied in relation to the same question.   (40 marks)

OR

2. 'We are all products of our environment.'

   Consider the texts you have studied for your comparative course in the light of this statement. Support the points made by reference to the texts you have chosen.   (70 marks)

B THE GENERAL VISION AND VIEWPOINT

1. There are certain key moments which highlight the author's general vision and viewpoint.

   (a) With reference to **one** of the texts you have studied for your comparative course, discuss this statement, referring to at least two key moments.   (30 marks)
   (b) Compare the key moments of the **two other** texts you have studied in the light of the above assessment.   (40 marks)

OR

2. 'The author's general vision of life is subtly revealed throughout the text.'

   Discuss this statement in relation to two or more texts you have studied for your comparative course.   (70 marks)

Sample 2

SECTION III

POETRY (70 marks)

Candidates must answer **A** – Unseen Poem **and B** – Prescribed Poetry.

A UNSEEN POEM (20 marks)

Answer **either** Question **1** or Question **2**.

Robert Hayden, American Poet Laureate from 1975–79, was the first African-American writer to be awarded this honour. He was born in 1913 in a poor area of Detroit. His childhood was unhappy and troubled. Many of Hayden's poems are about the traumas and tensions of family life. In this poem, he explores the past and present attitude of the speaker towards the dutiful role of a parent.

Those Winter Sundays

Sundays too my father got up early
and put his clothes on in the blueblack cold,
then with cracked hands that ached
from labour in the weekday weather made
banked fires blaze. No one ever thanked him.

I'd wake and hear the cold splintering, breaking.
When the rooms were warm, he'd call,
and slowly I would rise and dress,
fearing the chronic angers of that house.

Speaking indifferently to him,
who had driven out the cold
and polished my good shoes as well.
What did I know, what did I know
of love's austere and lonely offices?

Robert Hayden

1. What feelings towards the father, both past and present, are portrayed in this poem? In your answer, trace the portrayal of the feelings you describe through the poem's three stanzas.   (20 marks)

OR

2. Reread the poem carefully and point out the details that tell you about both the physical and emotional harshness of life in this household.   (20 marks)

B. PRESCRIBED POETRY (50 marks)

Candidates must answer **one** of the following questions (**1 – 4**).

1. **W.B. Yeats**
    'Yeats is a poet of great depth and beauty.'

    Discuss this statement with suitable reference to the poems of W.B. Yeats that you have studied.

2. **Adrienne Rich**
    'In her poetry Adrienne Rich gives us a deep insight into her own life.'

    Write an essay in which you would agree/disagree with this assessment. Support your answer with close reference to the poems of Rich that you have studied.

3. **T.S. Eliot**
    'T.S. Eliot reflects the uncertainty of modern life in his poetry.'

    Write a response to this statement, supporting your answer with appropriate reference to and quotations from the poems on your course.

4. **John Keats**
    'Introducing John Keats'

    Write an introduction to the poetry of the romantic poet John Keats that might appear in a school magazine.

Sample 2

LEAVING CERTIFICATE EXAMINATION

English – Higher Level – Paper I

SAMPLE PAPER 3

Total Marks: 200

Time: 2 hours 50 minutes

- This paper is divided into two sections,
  Section I COMPREHENDING and Section II COMPOSING.
- The paper contains **four** texts on the general theme of RELATIONSHIPS.
- Candidates should familiarise themselves with each of the texts before
  beginning their answers.

- Both sections of this paper (COMPREHENDING and COMPOSING) must be
  attempted.
- Each section carries 100 marks.

SECTION I – COMPREHENDING

- Two questions, A and B, follow each text.
- Candidates must answer a Question A on one text and a Question B on a
  different text. Candidates must answer only one Question A and only one
  Question B.
- **N.B.** Candidates may NOT answer a Question A and a Question B on the
  same text.

SECTION II – COMPOSING

Candidates must write on **one** of the compositions 1–7.

SECTION I
COMPREHENDING (100 marks)

TEXT 1

The following extract is the opening of Nigel Williams' comic novel *The Wimbledon Poisoner*.

Henry Farr did not, precisely, decide to murder his wife. It was simply that he could think of no other way of prolonging her absence from him indefinitely.

He had quite often, in the past, when she was being more than usually irritating, had fantasies about her death. She hurtled over cliffs in flaming cars or was brutally murdered on her way to the dry cleaners. But Henry was never actually responsible for the event. He was at the graveside looking mournful and interesting. Or he was coping with his daughter as she roamed the now deserted house, trying not to look as if he was glad to have the extra space. But he was never actually the instigator.

Once he had got the idea of killing her (and at first this fantasy did not seem very different from the reveries in which he wept by her open grave, comforted by young, fashionably dressed women) it took some time to appreciate that this scenario was of quite a different type from the others. It was a dream that could, if he so wished, become reality.

One Friday afternoon in September, he thought about strangling her. The Wimbledon Strangler. He liked that idea. He could see Edgar Lustgarten narrowing his eyes threateningly at the camera, as he paced out the length of Maple Drive. 'But Henry Farr,' Lustgarten was saying, 'with the folly of the criminal, the supreme arrogance of the murderer, had forgotten one vital thing. The shred of fibre that was to send Henry Farr to the gallows was – '

What was he thinking of? They didn't hang people any more. They wrote long, bestselling paperback books about them. Convicted murderers, especially brutal and disgusting ones, were followed around by as many *paparazzi* as the royal family. Their thoughts on life and love and literature were published in Sunday newspapers. Television documentary-makers asked them, respectfully, about exactly how they felt when they hacked their aged mothers to death or disembowelled a neighbour's child. This was the age of the murderer. And wasn't Edgar Lustgarten dead?

He wouldn't, anyway, be known as the Wimbledon Strangler, but as Henry Farr, cold-blooded psychopath. Or, better still, just Farr, cold-blooded psychopath. Henry liked the idea of being a cold-blooded psychopath. He pictured himself in a cell, as the television cameras rolled. He wouldn't moan and stutter and twitch the way most of these murderers did. He would give a clear, coherent account of how and why he had stabbed, shot, strangled, gassed or electrocuted her. 'Basically,' he would say to the camera, his gestures as urgent and incisive as those of any other citizen laying down the law on television, 'basically I'm a very passionate man. I love and I hate. And when love turns to hate, for me, you know, that's it. I simply had no wish for her to live. I stand by that decision.' Here he would suddenly stare straight into the camera lens in the way he had seen so many politicians do, and say, 'I challenge any red-blooded Englishman who really feels. Who has passion. Not to do the same. When love dies, it dies.'

Hang on. Was he a red-blooded Englishman or a cold-blooded psychopath? Or was he a bit of both? Was it possible to combine the two roles?

Either way, however he did it (and he was becoming increasingly sure that it was a good idea), his life was going to be a lot more fun. Being a convicted murderer had the edge on being a solicitor for Harris, Harris and Overdene of Blackfriars, London. Even Wormwood Scrubs must have more to offer, thought Henry as he rattled the coffee machine on the third floor, than Harris, Harris and Overdene. It wouldn't be so bad, somehow, if he was any good at being a solicitor. But, as Elinor was always telling him, Henry did not inspire confidence as a representative of the legal profession. He had, she maintained, a shifty look about him. 'How could you expect anyone to trust you with their conveyancing?' she had said to him, only last week. 'You look as if you've only just been let out on parole!'

(386 words)

N.B. **Candidates may NOT answer Question A and Question B on the same text.**
Questions A and B carry 50 marks each.

Question A

(i) Based upon your reading of this extract, write a character sketch (about 150 words) describing Henry Farr and the life he leads. (15)

(ii) What impression do you have of the relationship between Henry and his wife, and of her feelings towards him? (15)

(iii) From your reading of this passage, write a paragraph describing Nigel Williams' writing style. (20)

Question B

Write approximately 200 words continuing the above extract. (50)

TEXT 2
Keeping His Love

This is one of many articles written by Vera Brittain about the relationships between men and women in the aftermath of World War I and the Votes-for-women movement. She was one of the earliest women to study at Oxford but left her studies in 1915 to become a volunteer nurse tending the war-wounded. She was a very able writer and thinker on many social and political issues and is best known for her autobiographical work, *Testament of Youth*.

The other day my attention was arrested by an article in one of those popular little magazines with coloured covers which are now appearing in such large numbers to tempt the slender purse of the 'home woman'. The article was entitled 'Keeping House for Him', and opened as follows:

> The career of the homeworker is the finest in the world. If you can keep your husband's house efficiently, you an also keep his love ... Every wife is ambitious for her husband, and, when you come to think of it, a lot depends on her. She has to do with his smart appearance and his punctuality, her cooking makes a great difference to his health, and if she is a cheerful, happy little woman as well as a careful manager, he will be able to go to work free of all home worries.

I can see thousands of 'little women' – to say nothing of their husbands and their critical mothers-in-law – reading over these sugary-sweet sentiments with murmurs of purring approval. Like the writer of the article, they gladly take for granted that, because the work and the objects of the woman-in-the-little-house coincide so exactly with the description here given, they always will and always ought so to coincide. How many of these readers, I wonder, perceive the flagrantly immoral assumptions underlying these childishly innocent paragraphs? Perhaps we can help them to see by a brief analysis.

The first and fundamental assumption made is that a husband, in relation to his wife, is not a rational human being but a peculiarly exacting animal, whose love, which at best is cupboard love, has to be 'kept' by good food, creature comforts, and the same kind of protection against all worries as a too-conscientious mother arranges for her child.

According to assumption number two, a wife is a person without a life of her own. All her activities are second-hand, directed to a career, the appearance, the health, and the punctuality of another person.

Assumption number three impresses upon the 'little woman' that home responsibilities – which include some of the most important problems of life, such as the health and education of children –are not mutual burdens to be lightened for each by being shared with the other. The husband is to be 'spared' them, and the wife, whether competent or not, has to shoulder them all.

Fourthly, the wife is never to be herself, at ease with her husband as one may be at ease with a good, understanding friend. She is always to be acting, pretending to cheerfulness, and concealing difficulties and which her husband has the first right to be acquainted. In other words, throughout her married life she is to play the part of a first-class hypocrite.

Finally, such a marriage can never even approach a happy comradeship based on mutual confidence and respect. It is an employer and employee relation of the worst type, in which the employer is irrational, impatient, unadaptable, and at the mercy of quite unpredictable moods, while the employee receives no wages beyond her keep, and is unprotected by trade union regulations in a most exacting task.

(448 words)

N.B.   Candidates may NOT answer Question A and Question B on the same text.
Questions A and B carry 50 marks each.

Question A

(i)   Explain clearly why this writer disapproves of the ideas expressed in the magazine from which she quotes. (15)

(ii)   Vera Brittain's article was published early in the twentieth century. Do you think it is now outdated or does it have relevance for today's readers? Give reasons for your answer. (15)

(iii)   Do you think Vera Brittain argues her case well in this passage? Give reasons for your answer. (20)

Question B

Write an article for a popular magazine entitled, "My response to the views expressed by Vera Brittain." (50)

TEXT 3

The following monologue comes from Brian Friel's play *Faith Healer*. The speaker, Grace Hardy is sitting in a bare room at a small table. She is remembering the birth of her stillborn baby and its sad, lonely burial in a desolate field near Kinlochbervie, a Scottish village. Her husband Frank, was a travelling faith healer, and Teddy was his manager. At the time of the birth, they were travelling from one venue to another in an old van. Frank later abandons Grace, leaving Teddy to look after her.

GRACE (*quietly, almost dreamily*).
Kinlochbervie's where the baby's buried, two miles south of the village, in a field on the left hand side of the road as you go north. Funny isn't it, but I've never met anybody who's been to Kinlochbervie, not even Scottish people. But it *is* a very small village and very remote, right the way up in the north of Sutherland, about as far north as you can go in Scotland. And the people there told me that in good weather it is very beautiful and that you can see right across the sea to the Isle of Lewis in the Outer Hebrides. We just happened to be there and we were never there again and the week that we were there it rained all the time, not really rained but a heavy wet mist so that you could scarcely see across the road. But I'm sure it is a beautiful place in good weather. Anyhow, that's where the baby's buried, in Kinlochbervie in Sutherland, in the north of Scotland. Frank made a wooden cross to mark the grave and painted it white and wrote across it *Infant Child of Francis and Grace Hardy* – no name of course, because it was stillborn – just *Infant Child*. And I'm sure that cross is gone by now because it was a fragile thing and there were cows in the field and it wasn't a real cemetery anyway. And I had the baby in the back of the van and there was no nurse or doctor so no one knew anything about it except Frank and Teddy and me. And there was no clergyman at the graveside – Frank just said a few prayers that he made up. So there is no record of any kind. And he never talked about it afterwards; never once mentioned it again; and because he didn't, neither did I. So that was it. Over and done with. A finished thing. Yes. But I think it's a nice name Kinlochbervie – a complete sound – a name you wouldn't forget easily.

(338 words)

N.B. Candidates may NOT answer Question A and Question B on the same text.
Questions A and B carry 50 marks each.

Question A

(i) How much does Grace tell the audience about Kinlochbervie and what it was like when she was there? How does she like to imagine it now? (15)

(ii) Midway through the monologue, she begins to talk about Frank. What is your impression of him and of her feelings towards him from what she says? (15)

(iii) What do you think are Grace's feelings about her baby and the way in which it was buried? Support your answer by close reference to the text. (20)

Question B

Imagine a character in a play, many years after an important event in his/her life, reminiscing and reflecting upon that event. Write a monologue revealing the character's thoughts and feelings. (50)

TEXT 4
Scene of Modern Life

N.B. Candidates may NOT answer Question A and Question B on the same text.
Questions A and B carry 50 marks each.

Question A

  (i)   Write a factual description of this photograph. (10)

 (ii)   What image of young men and women in modern life is being presented here? Pay close attention to details in the photograph in your answer. (10)

(iii)   In what kind of publication would you expect to see this kind of visual image and what would you expect to be its purpose? (10)

(iv)   Imagine you are the photographer on this shoot. Write a note (about 100 words) to the four models explaining the look you want from this photograph, how you want **them** to look and the target audience to whom you wish to appeal. (20)

Question B

Write a text to accompany this visual. Explain clearly where you intend your text to be published. (50)

SECTION II
COMPOSING (100 marks)

Write a composition on **any one** of the following.
Each composition carries 100 marks.

The composition assignments below are intended to reflect language study in the areas of information, argument, persuasion, narration and the aesthetic use of language.

1. "I think it's a nice name Kinlochbervie – a complete sound – a name you wouldn't forget easily." (TEXT 3)

   Write a personal essay about a place that has meant a lot to you, explaining why you feel as you do about this place.

2. **TEXT 4 shows a scene from contemporary life. Write a features page for a newspaper describing the differences between the life expected by this generation and the life experienced by their parents.**

3. **Write a debate speech in which you attempt to persuade your listeners that "Married couples today have a greater chance of happiness than at any time in the past."**

4. **Write a personal essay in which you outline your views on the ideal relationship between parents and children.**

5. "Henry did not inspire confidence as a representative of the legal profession." (TEXT 1)

   Write a short story, opening with this scene.

6. "Happy comradeship based on mutual confidence and respect." (TEXT 2)

   Write a composition giving your views on a happy marital relationship.

7. "As he paced out the length of Maple Drive."

   Write a descriptive account of a day in the life of a suburban street.

LEAVING CERTIFICATE EXAMINATION

English – Higher Level – Paper 2

SAMPLE PAPER 3

Total Marks: 200

Time: 3 hours 20 minutes

Candidates must attempt the following:

- **ONE** question in SECTION I – The Single Text
- **ONE** question from SECTION II – The Comparative Study
- **ONE** question on the Unseen Poem from SECTION III – Poetry
- **ONE** question on Prescribed Poetry from SECTION III – Poetry

N.B. Candidates must answer on Shakespearean Drama.
They may do so in SECTION I, The Single Text (*King Lear*)
OR in SECTION II, The Comparative Study (*King Lear, The Tempest*).

INDEX OF SINGLE TEXTS

SECTION I

SINGLE TEXT (60 marks)

Candidates must answer **one** question from this section (**A–E**).

A   WUTHERING HEIGHTS — Emily Brontë

(i)   'Wuthering Heights is a love story of epic proportions.'

Consider this statement, supporting your answer with suitable reference to the text.

OR

(ii)   'The natural setting and the theme of nature add greatly to our understanding of Emily Brontë's *Wuthering Heights*.'

Discuss this statement with the aid of suitable reference to the text.

B   DANCING AT LUGHNASA — Brian Friel

(i)   'The Christian and the Pagan worlds collide in the village of Ballybeg.'

Would you agree with this statement? Support your answer with close reference to the drama.

OR

(ii)   'Friel uses many dramatic techniques to great effect in his play *Dancing at Lughnasa*.'

Discuss the author's dramatic approach, supporting your answer with suitable reference to the text.

C   KING LEAR — William Shakespeare

(i)   'The Gods are just.'

Do you agree with Edgar's assessment of divine justice in the play as a whole? Discuss this view in relation to the role of the Gods in *King Lear*.

OR

(ii)   'There are many similarities between the characters of Lear and Gloucester, but Lear's death is much more tragic.'
Consider both characters in the light of this statement, supporting your answers by suitable reference to the text.

D   THE GRAPES OF WRATH — John Steinbeck

(i)   'Ma Joad is a strong character who holds the family together on their journey to and time spent in California.'

Discuss this statement, supporting your answer with suitable reference to the text.

OR

(ii)   'In this bleak novel Steinbeck is on the side of the migrant workers as he condemns the landowners and those in authority.'

Consider this statement, supporting your answer with suitable reference to *The Grapes of Wrath*.

E   THE BLACKWATER LIGHTSHIP — Colm Tóibín

(i)   'Tóibín has crafted an unmissable read.'

Write a detailed review of *The Blackwater Lightship* that includes an evaluation of what you consider to be the most important aspects of the novel.

OR

(ii)   'Tóibín reveals Irish family life as "a web spun with guilt and tangled love".'

Discuss the novel in the light of this statement, supporting your answer with suitable reference to the text.

SECTION II

COMPARATIVE STUDY (70 marks)

Candidates must answer **one** question from **either A** – Literary Genre **or B** – The Cultural Context.

In your answer you may not use the text you have answered on in **Section I** – The Single Text.

N.B. The questions use the word **text** to refer to all the different kinds of texts available for study on this course, i.e. novel, play, short story, autobiography, biography, travel writing and film. The questions use the word **author** to refer to novelists, playwrights, writers in all genres, and film directors.

A LITERARY GENRE

1. (a) From **a text** you have studied as part of your comparative course, discuss the way in which the author has told his or her story. (30 marks)

    (b) Compare **two other texts** from your comparative course in the light of the statement in part (a). (40 marks)

OR

2. 'Authors approach their stories in different ways.'

    Basing your answer on the texts you have studied for you comparative course, compare and contrast the ways your chosen authors told their stories. (70 marks)

B THE CULTURAL TEXT

1. 'Each character emerges from a specific cultural context.' (70 marks)

    (a) Discuss this statement with reference to **one text** you studied for your comparative course. (30 marks)

    (b) Show how this statement is also relevant to **two other texts** on your comparative course. (40 marks)

OR

2. 'The way a society treats its members is central to many narratives.'

    Discuss the role and importance of society in **at least two of the texts** you have studied for your comparative course. (70 marks)

SECTION III

POETRY (70 marks)

Candidates must answer **A** – Unseen Poem **and B** – Prescribed Poetry.

A. UNSEEN POEM (20 marks)

Answer **either** Question **1** or Question **2**.

Grace Paley was born in the Bronx in 1922. She is best known for her short stories and for her campaigning work in anti-war and anti-nuclear movements but she has also published three poetry collections. She says about writing poetry:

'You have two ears. One ear is that literary ear... with us when we write in the tradition of English writing ... But there is something else ... and that is the ear of the language of home, and the language of your street and your own people.'

I Gave Away That Kid

I gave away that kid like he was an old button
  Here old button get off of me
  I don't need you anymore
  go on get out of here
  get into the army
  sew yourself onto the colonel's shirt
  or the captain's fly jackass
  don't you have any sense
  don't you read the papers
  why are you leaving now?

That kid walked out of here like he was the cat's
    pyjamas
  what are you wearing p j's for you damn fool?
  why are you crying you couldn't
  get another job here anyways
  go march to the army's drummer
  be a man like all your dead uncles
  then think of something else to do

Lost him, sorry about that the president said
  he was a good boy
  never see one like him again
  why don't you repeat that your honour
  why don't you sizzle up the meaning
  of that sentence for your breakfast
  why don't you stick him in a prayer
  and count to ten before my wife gets you.

That boy is a puddle in Beirut the paper says
  scraped up for singing in a church
  too bad too bad is a terrible tune
  It's no song at all how come you sing it?

I gave away that kid like he was an old button
  Here old button get offa me
  I don't need you anymore
  go on get out of here
  get into the army
  sew yourself onto the colonel's shirt
  or the captain's fly jackass
  don't you have any sense
  don't you read the papers
  why are you leaving now?

Grace Paley

---

1. Who do you think is speaking in this poem and about whom is this person speaking? What feelings is the speaker expressing in the poem? (20 marks)

OR

2. What attitudes to captains, colonels, the army and the president are expressed in the poem? Where are these attitudes made clear? (20 marks)

B PRESCRIBED POETRY (50 marks)

Candidates must answer **one** of the following questions (**1 – 4**).

1. **Eavan Boland**

    Write a personal response to the poetry of Eavan Boland.

2. **Derek Walcott**

    Discuss the view that Walcott's themes and imagery have a powerful impact and leave a lasting impression.

    Support your answer with suitable reference and/or quotation.

3. **Adrienne Rich**

    Outline your reasons for liking/disliking the poetry of Adrienne Rich.

    Support your answer with suitable reference to the poems of Rich on your course.

4. **T.S. Eliot**

    'Eliot's themes and language are introspective and modern.'

    Write an article for a school literary magazine introducing the poetry of T.S. Eliot.

LEAVING CERTIFICATE EXAMINATION

English – Higher Level – Paper I

SAMPLE PAPER 4

Total Marks: 200

Time: 2 hours 50 minutes

- This paper is divided into two sections,
  Section I COMPREHENDING and Section II COMPOSING.
- The paper contains **four** texts on the general theme of WRITERS and CHILDHOOD.
- Candidates should familiarise themselves with each of the texts before beginning their answers.

- Both sections of this paper (COMPREHENDING and COMPOSING) must be attempted.
- Each section carries 100 marks.

SECTION I – COMPREHENDING

- Two questions, A and B, follow each text.
- Candidates must answer a Question A on one text and a Question B on a different text. Candidates must answer only one Question A and only one Question B.
- **N.B.** Candidates may NOT answer a Question A and a Question B on the same text.

SECTION II – COMPOSING

Candidates must write on **one** of the compositions 1–7.

TEXT 1

My Mother

Alice Walker was the youngest of eight children born in 1944 to a sharecropping Mississippi family. She is best known for her book *The Color Purple* which won the Pulitzer Prize in 1983. The extract below comes from her autobiographical work, *In Search of Our Mothers' Gardens*. In it, you can see her love and admiration for a woman who was wonderfully creative, ambitious and determined in her survival of harsh times.

Five children later, I was born. And this is how I came to know my mother: she seemed a large, soft, loving-eyed woman who was rarely impatient in our home. Her quick, violent temper was on view only a few times a year, when she battled with the white landlord who had the misfortune to suggest to her that her children did not need to go to school.

She made all the clothes we wore, even my brothers' overalls. She made all the towels and sheets we used. She spent the summers canning vegetables and fruits. She spent the winter evenings making quilts to cover all our beds.

During the "working" day, she laboured beside — not behind — my father in the field. Her day began before sunup, and did not end until late at night. There was never a moment for her to sit down, undisturbed, to unravel her own private thoughts; never a time free from interruption — by work or the noisy inquiries of her many children. And yet, it is to my mother — and all our mothers who are not famous — that I went in search of the secret of what has fed that muzzled and often mutilated, but vibrant creative spirit that the black woman has inherited, and that pops out in wild and unlikely places to this day.

Like Mem, a character in *The Third Life of Grange Copeland*, my mother adorned with flowers whatever shabby house we were forced to live in. And not just your typical straggly country stand of zinnias, either. She planted ambitious gardens — and still does — with over fifty different varieties of plants that bloom profusely from early March until late November. Before she left home for the fields, she watered her flowers, chopped up the grass, and laid out new beds. When she returned from the fields she might divide clumps of bulbs, dig a cold pit, uproot and replant roses, or prune branches from her taller bushes or trees — until night came and it was too dark to see.

Whatever she planted grew as if by magic, and her fame as a grower of flowers spread over three counties. Because of her creativity with her flowers, even my memories of poverty are seen through a screen of blooms — sunflowers, petunias, roses, dahlias, forsythia, spirea, delphiniums, verbena ... and on and on.

And I remember people coming to my mother's yard to be given cuttings from her flowers; I hear again the praise showered on her because whatever rocky soil she landed on, she turned into a garden. A garden so brilliant with colours, so original in its design, so magnificent with life and creativity, that to this day people drive by our house in Georgia — perfect strangers and imperfect strangers — and ask to stand or walk among my mother's art.

I notice that it is only when my mother is working in her flowers that she is radiant, almost to the point of being invisible — except as Creator: hand and eye. She is involved in work her soul must have. Ordering the universe in the image of her personal conception of Beauty.

(528 words)

N.B. Candidates may NOT answer Question A and Question B on the same text.
Questions A and B carry 50 marks each.

Question A

(i) "Whatever rocky soil she landed on she turned into a garden." Explain how the writer has led us up to this statement and then uses it as a metaphor for her mother's life. (10)

(ii) As she looks back on her childhood from an adult perspective, what are the writer's feelings towards her mother? (10)

(iii) What is your understanding of the final paragraph in the passage? (10)

(iv) What do you learn about Alice Walker from reading this passage? (20)

Question B

Write the opening paragraphs (150–200 words) of an autobiographical essay in which a writer portrays either a mother or father to the reader. (50)

TEXT 2

The following two images are taken from the video cover of Giuseppi Tornatore's film *Cinema Paradiso*. They show Toto, the young boy who is the film's central character and Alfredo, the local cinema projectionist who is a kindly man and a formative influence on his life. World War II has ended and Toto's father has died on the Russian Front. The film very beautifully portrays Toto's poor Catholic childhood in the little Sicilian town of Giancalda where the local cinema and the world of film are his boyhood fascination.

N.B.   Candidates may NOT answer Question A and Question B on the same text.
        Questions A and B carry 50 marks each.

Question A

(i)   Write a factual description of these two images. (10)

(ii)   From what you see in the photographs, what impression of the life and character of the little boy do you have? (10)

(iii) How do these images convey the impression of Alfredo's importance in the boy's life and the film? (10)

(iv)   What impression of the film is conveyed in the short pieces of text on the visual images? (10)

(v)   In what sense do the two pictures present contrasting images? (10)

Question B

Write a review for a magazine which is to be distributed free to households in your area, of a film you recently saw. (50)

TEXT 3

The Joyce Family

This passage is taken from Richard Ellmann's award-winning 1959 biography of James Joyce. It portrays the Joyce family around the year 1895. Due to the extravagance and idleness of their father, John Joyce, the ten children and their mother, May, were living in very poor rented accommodation in North Richmond Street in the inner city. James was at school in Belvedere where he had been given a scholarship.

The Joyce sons were beginning to attain separate individualities. John Stanislaus Joyce, Jr., known as 'Stannie,' was a serious, round-headed boy, heavy-set though athletic, and shorter by several inches than James; he already gave good signs of the bluntness and determination that were to characterize his life. The next brother, Charles, was to prove jaunty and capricious, a boy of many careers, with little ability for any of them. The youngest boy was George, who showed signs of his oldest brother's wit and intelligence, but had only a few years to live. Among the girls the personalities were less distinct; Margaret, the oldest, approximated her mother's gentle steadfastness, and played the piano well. Eileen was more excitable and less ordered; Mary ('May') was quiet and pacific; Eva and Florence were withdrawn, Florence especially; while Mabel, the youngest, was unexpectedly merry. Almost all were capable on occasion of those sudden insights that endow their decay as a family with unexpected distinction.

The prevailing tone in the family was male; the girls, 'my twenty-three sisters,' as James Joyce once called them, had a very subordinate place and, frightened by their father's rebukes, did not attempt to assert themselves. Among the boys the emphasis fell strongly on James at the expense of the others; it was James for whom John Joyce, his friends, and most of the relatives freely predicted a great career in some as yet undetermined profession. Stanislaus, almost three years younger but closest to James in age and understanding, trailed him worshipfully. He preferred to study what James studied rather than what Belvedere College prescribed, and so methodically pursued his brother into European literature at the expense of his own grades.

John Joyce, fearsome and jovial by turns, kept the family's life from being either comfortable or tedious. In his better moods he was their comic: at breakfast one morning, for example, he read from the *Freeman's Journal* the obituary notice of a friend, Mrs. Cassidy. May Joyce was shocked and cried out, 'Oh! Don't tell me that Mrs. Cassidy is dead.' 'Well, I don't quite know about that,' replied John Joyce, eyeing his wife solemnly through his monocle, 'but someone has taken the liberty of burying her.' James burst into laughter, repeated the joke later to his schoolmates, and still later to the readers of *Ulysses*.

On Sunday mornings John Joyce busied himself hurrying the rest of the family off to mass, while he stayed home himself. When his two eldest sons returned he often took them for a walk. His undisguised preference for James reduced Stanislaus's pleasure in such promenades, but James was indulgent and fascinated by the little dapper man with his straw hat. John Joyce spoke to them of Dublin characters, he pointed out where Swift once lived, where Addison walked, where Sir William Wilde had his surgery. He knew all the stories, inside and out; besides what he picked up from other sources, he retained from his days as a rate collector the most savoury details of Dublin's private life.

(522 words)

N.B. Candidates may NOT answer Question A and Question B on the same text.
Questions A and B carry 50 marks each.

Question A

(i) From your reading of this passage, characterise the relationship between John Joyce and his eldest son, James. (15)

(ii) Outline the character of John Joyce and his relationship with his other children. (15)

(iii) Do you think this is a well-written portrayal of a family and its relationships? Give reasons for your answer. (20)

Question B

Your school has been twinned with an American High School. You have been asked to write 200 words entitled "The average Irish family today". The aim is to give students in the U.S. school an impression of ordinary Irish family life. Write the piece which you think would give an accurate picture. (50)

Sample 4

TEXT 4

Mossbawn

The following passage is taken from *Mossbawn*, one of Seamus Heaney's reminiscences of his childhood. This piece is published in book form but has also been broadcast on radio, so you can imagine it being read aloud and written as much for the ear of the listener as for the eye of the solitary reader.

I do not know what age I was when I got lost in the pea-drills in a field behind the house, but it is a half-dream to me, and I've heard about it so often that I may even be imagining it. Yet, by now, I have imagined it so long and so often that I know what it was like: a green web, a caul of veined light, a tangle of rods and pods, stalks and tendrils, full of assuaging earth and leaf smell, a sunlit lair. I'm sitting as if just wakened from a winter sleep and gradually become aware of voices, coming closer, calling my name, and for no reason at all I have begun to weep.

All children want to crouch in their secret nests. I loved the fork of a beech tree at the head of our lane, the close thicket of a boxwood hedge in the front of the house, the soft, collapsing pile of hay in a back corner of the byre; but especially I spent time in the throat of an old willow tree at the end of the farmyard. It was a hollow tree, with gnarled, spreading roots, a soft, perishing bark and a pithy inside. Its mouth was like the fat and solid opening of a horse's collar, and, once you squeezed in through it, you were at the heart of a different life, looking out on the familiar yard as if it were suddenly behind a pane of strangeness. Above your head, the living tree flourished and breathed, you shouldered the slightly vibrant bole, and if you put your forehead to the rough pith you felt the whole lithe and whispering crown of willow moving in the sky above you. In that tight cleft, you sensed the embrace of light and branches, you were a little Atlas shouldering it all, a little Cerunnos pivoting a world of antlers.

The world grew. Mossbawn, the first place, widened. There was what we called the Sandy Loaning, a sanded pathway between old hedges leading off the road, first among fields and then through a small bog, to a remote farmhouse. It was a silky, fragrant world there, and for the first few hundred yards you were safe enough. The sides of the lane were banks of earth topped with broom and ferns, quilted with moss and primroses. Behind the broom, in the high grass, cattle munched reassuringly. Rabbits occasionally broke cover and ran ahead of you in a flurry of dry sand. There were wrens and goldfinches. But, gradually, those lush and definite fields gave way to scraggy marshland. Birch trees stood up to their pale shins in swamps. The ferns thickened above you. Scuffles in old leaves made you nervous and you dared yourself always to pass the badger's set, a wound of fresh mould in an overgrown ditch where the old brock had gone to earth.

(314 words)

N.B.   Candidates may NOT answer Question A and Question B on the same text.
       Questions A and B carry 50 marks each.

Question A

(i)   Would you agree that the opening paragraph is a very sensuous childhood memory? Give reasons for your answer. (10)

(ii) "All children love to crouch in their secret nests." Show how the writer goes on to develop this statement in the second paragraph. (10)

(iii) The third paragraph expands the memories and the journey. What new elements are introduced here? (10)

(iv) What impression of the personality of the writer do you have from the memories he presents in this passage? (10)

(v)   What do you think are the writer's feelings for this childhood place? How are his feelings made known to the reader? (10)

Question B

Write the opening (150–200 words) of a novel aimed at 9–10 year old children describing a place that is important to a young child. (50)

SECTION II
COMPOSING (100 marks)

Write a composition on **any one** of the following.
Each composition carries 100 marks.

The composition assignments below are intended to reflect language study in the areas of information, argument, persuasion, narration and the aesthetic use of language.

1. "A garden so brilliant with colors, so original in its design, so magnificent with life and creativity…"
   (TEXT 1)

   Compose a tale entitled *A Garden so Brilliant* inspired by the lines above.

2. TEXT 2 shows a child, who in his adult life would become a film director, looking with delight at a reel of film.

   Write a personal essay recalling happy childhood memories of a person, place or event which was very important to you in your formative years.

3. "He read from *The Freeman's Journal* the obituary notice of a friend."

   Newspapers publish obituaries of interesting people who have recently died, giving information about their lives and achievements. Write an obituary of a person, who may be real or imaginary, for inclusion in a newspaper's obituary page.

4. "Stanislaus, almost three years younger but closest to James in age and understanding, trailed him worshipfully."

   Write a composition describing a childhood friendship in which one child is in awe of another.

5. "It was a hollow tree, with gnarled, spreading roots, a soft, perishing bark and a pithy inside."

   Write a story, using this as your opening sentence.

6. "She battled with the white landlord who had the misfortune to suggest to her that her children did not need to go to school."

   Write a political speech in which you argue that the key to a better society is more spending on education.

7. "To this day people drive by our house in Georgia ... and ask to stand or walk among my mother's art.
   (TEXT 1)

   Write an article for your local Resident's Newsletter, persuading householders that everyone should put effort into gardening in the coming season.

LEAVING CERTIFICATE EXAMINATION

English – Higher Level – Paper 2

SAMPLE PAPER 4

Total Marks: 200

Time: 3 hours 20 minutes

Candidates must attempt the following:

- **ONE** question in SECTION I – The Single Text
- **ONE** question from SECTION II – The Comparative Study
- **ONE** question on the Unseen Poem from SECTION III – Poetry
- **ONE** question on Prescribed Poetry from SECTION III – Poetry

N.B. Candidates must answer on Shakespearean Drama.
They may do so in SECTION I, The Single Text *(King Lear)*
OR in SECTION II, The Comparative Study *(King Lear, The Tempest)*.

INDEX OF SINGLE TEXTS

SECTION I

SINGLE TEXT (60 marks)

Candidates must answer **one** question from this section (A–E).

A   WUTHERING HEIGHTS — Emily Brontë

(i)   Discuss the theme of Revenge in the novel *Wuthering Heights* by Emily Brontë. Support your views with suitable reference to the text.

OR

(ii) 'Heathcliff is not an inhuman monster, he is a victim of the circumstances of his upbringing.'

Discuss this assessment of the character of Heathcliff, one of literature's most compelling creations.

B   DANCING AT LUGHNASA — Brian Friel

(i)   Discuss the view, with reference to *Dancing at Lughnasa*, that 'Brian Friel is one of the most accomplished playwrights working in English today'.

Support your answer with suitable reference to the text.

OR

(ii) 'Both tragedy and comedy are at the heart of this dramatic work.'

Discuss this assessment with suitable reference to *Dancing at Lughnasa* by Brian Friel.

C   KING LEAR — William Shakespeare

(i)   'Goneril and Regan both fascinate and repel us with their "filial ingratitude".'

Do you agree with this assessment of Lear's daughters? Support your answer with suitable reference and/or quotation.

OR

(ii) 'Shakespeare's *King Lear* has many moments of compelling drama.'

Discuss the dramatic impact of the play in the light of the above statement.

D   THE GRAPES OF WRATH — John Steinbeck

(i)   Discuss the theme of 'Man's inhumanity to man' as portrayed in the novel *The Grapes of Wrath* by John Steinbeck.

OR

(ii) Discuss the role of Jim Casy in the novel *The Grapes of Wrath*.

Support your answer with suitable reference to the text.

E   THE BLACKWATER LIGHTSHIP — Colm Tóibín

(i)   'Family bonds and relationships are at the heart of Tóibín's *The Blackwater Lightship*.'

Discuss this view of the novel with suitable reference to the text.

OR

(ii) 'Tóibín's *Blackwater Lightship* is a quiet, sad, elegaic story.'

Write a detailed review of the novel in view of this assessment.

SECTION II

COMPARATIVE STUDY (70 marks)

Candidates must answer **one** question from **either A** – Literary Genre **or B** – The Cultural Context.

In your answer you may not use the text you have answered on in **Section I** – The Single Text.

N.B. The questions use the word **text** to refer to all the different kinds of texts available for study on this course, i.e. novel, play, short story, autobiography, biography, travel writing and film. The questions use the word **author** to refer to novelists, playwrights, writers in all genres, and film directors.

A   LITERARY GENRE

1. 'Each author brings his own unique style to the creation of a text.'
    (a) Compare **two of the texts** you have studied in your comparative course in the light of the above statement.   (40 marks)

    (b) Discuss **a third text** on your comparative with reference to part (a) above.   (30 marks)

OR

2. 'Telling a story is an art in itself.'

    In the light of this statement, compare the ways in which the texts on your comparative course told their stories.   (70 marks)

B   THE CULTURAL CONTEXT

1. (a) Choose any **one of the texts** you have studied as part of your comparative course and discuss how the cultural environment shapes the life of the individual.   (30 marks)

    (b) Compare **two other texts** from your comparative course in the light of the discussion in part (a) above.   (40 marks)

OR

2. Discuss the importance of the Cultural Context in the texts you have studied for your comparative course. You must deal with at least two texts.   (70 marks)

SECTION III

POETRY (70 marks)

Candidates must answer **A** – Unseen Poem **and B** – Prescribed Poetry.

A   UNSEEN POEM (20 marks)

Answer **either** Question **1** or Question **2**.

In this poem, Eiléan Ní Chuilleanáin describes standing with her mother in Italy in the Cathedral of Parma. They are looking up at the dome of the church, enjoying and admiring a painting of the Ascension of the Virgin Mary into Heaven. As she describes the painting in detail, we feel that the poet is telling us about something else as well. The words manage to do two things at once; they describe Mary ascending into heaven and they convey the poet's feelings of love for her mother and her grief after her death.

Fireman's Lift

I was standing beside you looking up
Through the big tree of the cupola
Where the church splits wide open to admit
Celestial choirs, the fall-out of brightness.

The Virgin was spiralling to heaven,
Hauled up in stages. Past mist and shining,
Teams of angelic arms were heaving,
Supporting, crowding her, and we stepped

Back, as the painter longed to
While his arm swept in the large strokes.
We saw the work entire, and how the light

Melted and faded bodies so that
Loose feet and elbows and staring eyes
Floated in the wide stone petticoat
Clear and free as weeds.

This is what love sees, that angle:
The crick in the branch loaded with fruit,
A jaw defining itself, a shoulder yoked,
The back making itself a roof
The legs a bridge, the hands,
A crane and a cradle.

Their heads bowed over to reflect on her
Fair face and hair so like their own
As she passed through their hands. We saw
    them
Lifting her, the pillars of their arms

(Her face a capital leaning into an arch)
As the muscles clung and shifted
For a final purchase together
Under her weight as she came to the edge of
    the cloud.

Eiléan Ní Chuilleanáin

1. Who are the 'I' and 'you' in this poem? What is the speaker remembering about herself, her companion and the scene they were observing in the opening four stanzas? In your answer, point out the words and phrases that particularly help you to visualise this scene as you read.

(20 marks)

OR

2. From your reading of this poem, what do you think are the feelings of the speaker for her mother? Where in the poem are these feelings best expressed?   (20 marks)

B PRESCRIBED POETRY (50 marks)

Candidates must answer **one** of the following questions (**1 – 4**).

1. **Patrick Kavanagh**

    Discuss the view that Patrick Kavanagh draws on personal experience, both good and bad, when crafting his poetry.

    Support your answer with suitable reference and/or quotation.

2. **Micahael Longley**

    'Longley's poems are inherently autobiographical.'

    Write a detailed response to the poetry of Michael Longley in the light of this statement. Support your discussion with suitable reference to the poems on your course.

3. **W.B. Yeats**

    Write a personal response to the poetry of Ireland's greatest poet, W.B. Yeats.

    Support points with suitable reference and/or quotation.

4. **John Keats**

    'The poetry of John Keats appeals to readers for various different reasons.'

    Write the text of a talk you would give to a group of fellow students in the light of the above statement. Support your points with suitable references to the poems of Keats you have studied.

REVISION BOOK ORDER FORM

**25% OFF
if you order by
November 27th**

Leaving Certificate

Part No.	Title	Quantity	Price	Total
BIOLRRH	Rapid Revision Biology (Higher Level) (Reville)		10.00	
BILRRO	Rapid Revision Biology (Ordinary Level) (Reville)		10.00	
BL997X	Essential Exam Revision Biology		9.95	
CHLCRR	Rapid Revision Chemistry		10.00	
PLRRP	Rapid Revision Physics		10.00	
HELRR	Rapid Revision Home Economics (New Edition)		10.00	
LRRF	Rapid Revision French Higher Level (Hogan)		10.00	
F6652	Rapid Revision French Ordinary Level (Hogan)		10.00	
ML0504	Rapid Revision Higher Level Maths (O'Brien)		9.95	
ML0294	Essential Revision Guide Maths (HL) (Kelly/Mills)		10.00	
HL1747	Essential Revision Guide to Maths (OL) (Kelly/Mills)		9.95	
GR7071	Rapid Revision Geography (Guilmartin)		9.95	
CLEBRR	Rapid Revision Business		9.95	
GA8140	Labhair Liom [Book + CD] LC Irish Oral		10.00	
AC1921	Rapid Revision Accounting (New Edition)		10.00	
EN7888	Rapid Revision English (HL) (Kelly)		9.95	
EL692X	English Essential Guide to Paper 1 Higher Level		9.95	
E4755	King Lear: An Exam Guide		7.95	
EC9025	Rapid Revision Economics (Ruane)		9.95	
FR0498	Courrier – Leaving Certificate French		9.95	
MU8974	Rapid Revision Music (Costello)		9.95	
AS1624	Rapid Revision Agricultural Science		9.95	
SP0306	Rapid Revision Spanish		14.99	

Junior Certificate

Part No.	Title	Quantity	Price	Total
HJHRR	Rapid Revision History		8.75	
EN6601	Rapid Revision English (OL) (John Scally)		8.75	
EJRREH	Rapid Revision English (HL) (John Scally)		9.95	
RJRRG	Religion – A Revision Guide		10.00	
AJPA	Project Art		14.50	
EJ0313	Examination Writing Skills for JC English		9.95	
FR1754	Expressions Françaises –Writing Skills		9.95	
FR7950	Cahier Clef		10.75	
GR1099	Rapid Revision Geography		9.95	
SP0283	Rapid Revision Spanish		9.95	
			Total	
			– 25% Discount	
			Amount Due	

Name:...

Address: ....

....

Post order plus cheque (payable to Folens) to Folens Publishers, Hibernian Industrial Estate, Greenhills Road,Tallaght, Dublin 24.
Customer service: 0818-FOLENS – 0818-365367; website: www.folens.ie